THESE ORDINARY
MOMENTS OF GRIEF

A Collection of Memories, Musings,
and Introspection

THESE ORDINARY MOMENTS OF GRIEF

A COLLECTION OF MEMORIES, MUSINGS, AND INTROSPECTION

D.C. ZHANG

NEW DEGREE PRESS
COPYRIGHT © 2021 D.C. ZHANG

THESE ORDINARY MOMENTS OF GRIEF

ISBN 979-8-88504-042-6 *Paperback*
979-8-88504-143-0 *Kindle Ebook*
979-8-88504-144-7 *Ebook*

To my mother, who will never know I wrote a book for her, and who I wish I didn't have to write this book for. You were amazing. You fought so hard for us.

TABLE OF CONTENTS

AUTHOR'S NOTE

"Friendship ... is born at the moment when one man says to another "What! You too? I thought that no one but myself..."

—C. S. LEWIS.

When I first started writing this memoir, I did not have a clear purpose in mind. I just knew what had suddenly motivated me to do so: COVID-19.

There is something about being in solitude that makes you restless. During this time, I saw that the people around me were building their own gardens, remodeling their homes, opening an Etsy shop, selling sourdough bread on Instagram, or starting their own YouTube channel. I wanted to produce something too, create something and release it into the world.

During this restlessness, a friend introduced me to New Degree Press and resurfaced my childhood daydream of being a writer. This could my chance to be the next J. K. Rowling—for me to realize my dream of becoming a young adult writer. Except I had no story.

All I had was the grief from losing my mother to ovarian cancer almost two years ago and the few social media posts

I wrote when I missed her too much and wanted the world to know.

Maybe, I could turn those long Instagram captions into the pages of a book.

From that idea, I catapulted into writing about grief without any clear direction. I dug into the grotto of my mind picking a memory, moment, or musing and pulled it out to examine, analyze, and put on display for my editors to see. All those encounters of grief and I had no idea how they were connected until my book positioning call. Despite never mentioning the word, my editor said, "It sounds like you were lonely."

Lonely.

Strange that a person I'd only talked to twice could recognize a loneliness in me that I couldn't see.

When you look at grief from far away, it looks like an intimidating knot made up of bad and terrible things tied and tangled together. It seems impossible to unravel, and it's only when you step closer that you begin to see how all the strands intertwine with each other. For the first time, I could see the thread of loneliness throughout.

When a loved one dies, your whole world changes. Everything changes. You are now carrying grief in their absence. In the beginning, I felt like people understood that I had gone through this life-altering change; after a while, it seemed like they thought I had returned to normal, to who I was before my mother died. Besides God, I felt like I was the only one who knew I was grieving.

I found my purpose. I had to let others know that I was grieving and what that felt like.

The more I wrote, the more I realized how tired I was all this time from holding my words in. I want to let my words roam free, to go as far as they can. When I see my words out in the open, for the world to see and acknowledge, I feel scared but also less lonely—like my grief is real, like all the things that go on in my head and heart matter.

To the grievers, I hope that if something in this book resonates with you, you will feel a little less lonely in that moment. You are not alone in what you feel, in what you went through. There are others like you.

To the not-yet grievers, I hope you will understand a little something about those of us who have experienced loss; we were never really that different from you. Do not be afraid of the grief we have in us.

Here are all the things I wanted to say but didn't, all the unsaid things I kept inside of me, everything I have been waiting to let out. These particular memories, musings, and introspections that I have curated over time into "ordinary moments of grief" are yours now.

Friend, I hope one day to come across your ordinary moments too because whether we want to or not, if we love anything, anyone, we will all have to carry grief with us.

CHAPTER 1

NOT JUST A WALK IN THE PARK

———

My house is conveniently located right across the park—or inconveniently if you don't like waking up Saturday mornings to the cheers of people playing cricket. Open to anyone who likes to play tennis, baseball, basketball, or on the playground, it is not surprising the park is a hot spot for neighborhood residents. Starting at 5 p.m. every day, I begin to hear bits and pieces of conversations from people as they walk past my house with their families.

At times, it seemed like everyone knew how to take advantage of the park except for the people living right next to it: my family. When I was younger, I lived in a neighborhood in Texas that did not have a park. The neighborhood kids and I would ride our bikes to and from each other's houses and in the cul-de-sac. We didn't need a park; we just needed each other and our bikes. Then, I moved to California, where I knew no one. All my friends lived in other neighborhoods, so I stayed indoors and spent my time reading or drawing, completely uninterested in the park.

My parents didn't care for the park either. Once they returned from working at a restaurant, they only had enough time to shower, eat dinner, and watch an episode of the Chinese drama playing on TV before heading straight to bed. They repeated this pattern six times a week, except for Sundays, which were reserved for church. Sunday afternoons would have been the perfect time to take a stroll if they weren't running errands that they couldn't do when they worked grueling ten-hours days. If my mother wasn't grocery shopping, gardening, or cleaning the house on Sunday afternoons, she would either be napping or shopping if she had the energy.

The park next to my house would have continued to be unappreciated and unnoticed if it weren't for the ovarian cancer.

Already a paranoid and anxious person pre-cancer, my mother became even more health obsessive and eccentrically germophobic. Before she became sick, she often told everyone to stand a few feet away from the microwave to avoid the radiation. After her diagnosis, she stopped using the microwave altogether, opting to reheat her food using the stove instead. I started seeing sea cucumbers, known for fighting cancer, in our fridge. My mother would insist we filter our water and then boil it. Or was it boil the water and then filter it? Either way, filtered water was no longer safe enough. Walking around the park was another healthy habit she picked up. After my mother finished her last round of chemotherapy, she walked religiously around the park in the morning, afternoon, and evening. Whether it was by exercising often or eating healthy food, she was determined to do everything she could to prevent her illness from returning.

Around the time she was first diagnosed, I had started working at a nonprofit agency that provided 24/7 service for people with developmental disabilities. I had to ensure that the homes were completely staffed before I clocked out. Since the agency was understaffed, I spent a majority of my time calling employees asking—sometimes begging—them to take extra shifts. By the time I came home, I was drained. I was ready to plop on the couch and mindlessly scroll through my phone, trying not to think about how I would have to go back to work the next day. I didn't want to talk to anyone and merely wanted to be left alone to waste time.

My mother never seemed to get this memo. I always appeared to get home right when my parents were heading out for their stroll. Seeing me, my mother would immediately ask me to join their evening ritual. Usually, I would shake my head no while they looked at me disapprovingly. I knew what they were thinking; they interpreted my destressing habit as laziness. Then, my mother would go on about the benefits of walking, how it would prolong my life, and how it could help me lose weight. My dad would say, "Let's just go, she never listens to us."

Suddenly, walking didn't feel like a leisure activity anymore, but a tool to call out my flaws.

One time, my mom was being especially persistent, so I gave in grudgingly. Like a teenager, I trailed behind my parents with my hands in my pockets, sighing and thinking back to how stressful my day was and how all I wanted was to melt into the couch at home. If I became a puddle like the witch in *The Wizard of Oz,* then I wouldn't have to go to work.

"Take your hands out of your pockets and swing them like me," my mom commanded from the front.

Scowling, I asked, "Why? I'm walking like you wanted me to. Can't I just walk the way I want to?"

"No, walking without your arms swinging doesn't count as exercising. You might as well not be walking," my mom called back.

Then I might as well go home.

My dad said nothing from between us, but his arms were swinging back and forth, mimicking my mom's.

"But I'm still moving." I called from the back a little loudly, hoping she would hear the frustration in my voice and take that as a cue to let me be.

She ignored me.

Defeated, I sighed and took my hands out of my pockets and swung them limply the rest of the way, the most that I could do to rebel. As we got closer to home, my mother asked if I wanted to walk around the park one more time. Depending on your pace, it would have taken another 10–15 minutes, time I didn't want to spare. All I wanted was to unwind, even if it was wasteful and unhealthy. I didn't want to give into another one of my mother's many health concerns.

I thought we would always have tomorrow. The park was still going to be there. And my mother would still insist that I walk with her. My parents would continue to conveniently take their stroll right when I came home from work. There would be plenty of opportunities to walk with them, and maybe next time, I wouldn't feel like I was forced to attend.

Unlike my mother, I did not think the cancer was going to come back. I thought we were safe—that after going through this trial, God wouldn't put us through another one so soon and so much more devastating. I thought we had conquered this battle, that the enemy was defeated, and that we didn't have to fight anymore. Somewhere along the way, I became convinced that we were invincible because of how smoothly her first encounter with cancer went. The surgery went well; her tests showed no signs of cancer after her chemotherapy. We were going to be okay.

However, the battles always turned out to be wars instead. Just because we won one didn't mean we were going to win them all in the end.

If I had known how things were going to be in a year or two, I would have said yes to going around the park many more times. All those 10–15 minutes I craved for myself could have been spent with her. If I went with her around the park twice every day, I would have had so many hours of time back with my mother, hours I lost doing nothing. I wish I knew how easy my mother made it for me to make her happy; a simple yes was all I needed to say. The irony was that walking would have helped relieve my stress so much more than spending time on my phone.

My mother eventually stopped walking around the park when her cancer returned aggressively the second time. Everything that went right the first time went wrong. Disappointment after disappointment. Defeat after defeat. There was no time for walking, only mourning the losses. Like her, my dad and I also stopped walking around the park until two weeks after my mother's funeral when we decided to take a stroll after dinner. I didn't think much of it at the time. I had forgotten how much my mother enjoyed walking by then; my mother only left the house the last six months of her life to go to clinical trials or treatments in Chinatown.

Forgetting how persistent my mother was about her walking routine, I looked forward to getting out of the house and getting some fresh air. As I kept walking, I suddenly felt my heart tightening up. I wasn't running or even walking fast.

My dad and I were keeping a slow pace, awkwardly walking next to each other. It felt strange that my dad was next to me. Usually, my dad would be a few steps ahead of me, trying to catch up with my mother. I looked ahead and realized that my mother was no longer walking briskly ahead of us.

Oh, so I wasn't out of shape. I was merely missing my mother.

I thought grief was supposed to hurt the most when your loved one dies or during the funeral. I didn't know that doing such an ordinary activity like taking a stroll in my neighborhood would hurt as much as notifying the hospice that my mother died or giving the eulogy at her funeral.

Funerals may signal the end of someone's life, but for grievers, they are the start of their new lives without their loved ones. Just like the hard work of marriage comes after the wedding, the hard work of grief comes after the funeral.

I didn't only endure my grief at her funeral but in all the ordinary moments that came afterwards. These moments were so trivial and insignificant before, but they became so much more painful and bittersweet without the person I love. What I hated most about these moments is how they came suddenly, overwhelming me, catching me off guard. I never know what will trigger a thought or moment of my mother. Even the happy moments make me feel sad.

This was the first ordinary moment of grief I encountered: the walk around the park with my father. In that moment, I realized how many more first experiences I would have to go through without my mother. I wanted to return home and not do anything for the first time without her. I wanted to go back, take back every single step without her. For so long, my family was a three-legged table, what were we supposed to do now with one leg gone? How could we keep standing?

How could we keep doing this ordinary activity now that she was gone?

Somehow, we kept going without her, not speaking. If this walk was as hard for me as it was for my dad, he never gave any indication. He just walked quietly next to me, keeping with my pace. Eventually we made it home. No one asked us if we wanted to walk around the park one more time.

I avoided the park for a while after that first walk without her. After some time, I found my way back when her loss wasn't so fresh. Sometimes, I would go with my father on a stroll if he asked and other times by myself. I was reminded of my mother's absence more when we made our way through the neighborhood together. There was no one leading us, just the open street ahead of us. No one was going to tell us to walk faster or to take our hands out of our pockets.

Eventually, walking around the park didn't hurt as much as the first time. Either I got used to the pain over time or the endorphins from moving around dulled the ache of my loss. Once the pandemic hit, I began to develop a newfound appreciation for the park. I needed a way to relieve my stress from work and from being home all day. So, I started to walk around the park routinely and very persistently since I recently started tracking my steps and giving myself milestones to reach. I will admit that I don't swing my arms as enthusiastically as my mother once did, but I do make the conscious effort to not keep my hands in my pockets at the very least.

I finally got around to doing what my mother wanted me to do. It took a pandemic for me to enjoy walking. But my mother was the same way; it took cancer for her to appreciate what our neighborhood had to offer.

How unfortunate our missed timing was. I wish we could have shared the enjoyment of this simple activity together, in the same timeline. Instead, she enjoyed her walks, while I saw it as something she made me do. I finally developed the habit of walking when she was gone; she had been unable to see the fruits of her labor. She was always right in the end, always knew what was better for me even when she wasn't alive to see it.

What other activities will I grow into that she isn't there to see?

While I am glad that I discovered this new hobby, I am disappointed at myself for being so late. I know I can't do anything about our timeline, but I can't help but wish I was less stubborn, less absorbed in myself. I know we all grow at our own pace, but my slowness cost me valuable time with my mother. When I calculate how much time I could have spent with my mother, I don't feel like forgiving my younger self.

I'm not usually this bitter toward myself. It is only because there is no one else to blame that I can't help but look at myself, thinking of all the ways I could have been a better daughter. I thought I would always have opportunities to appreciate her. There were so many things we didn't do together, weren't ready for. Time would have given us so many chances to grow into the same hobbies and to appreciate each other more.

Sometimes when I am walking along the same path she once took, I think about the last scene from *A Walk to Remember* where Landon, the main character, takes a walk by himself to a lake. He says internally to himself about the person he lost, "I will always miss her. But her love is like the wind. I can't see it, but I can feel it."

How incredibly cheesy.

But before I can stop myself, I start to build a similar dialogue and a voice suddenly says, "Can you picture your mother ahead of you? It's not that hard. Her back is towards you, and she's walking briskly ahead. It is almost like she is here with you right now." Suddenly a flashback of all the times my mother and I spent at the park plays in my head.

I really need to stop listening to soundtracks on my strolls or else I will keep picturing myself as the main character of a movie or show.

Even though I was the one who created that voice, I hate it because I feel the exact opposite. She is not here. She is gone. Picturing her in front of me won't bring her back. That is an illusion built on regret and guilt. I will never see my mother leading me around the park again. And nothing will make me feel like she is here with me. This is my grief every day—looking ahead and not seeing my mother.

A friend once told me, "Don't focus on the uncertain things, but the certain ones."

I don't know what kind of future we missed with her death. I can only speculate about all the things we were supposed to do together. But this is what I know: my mother loved me, and I know the exact path she took around the park. Over time, I learned that instead of fixating on her absence, I would focus on the details of what I saw on the path. Everything I saw—from the mailboxes on the streets, the same surrounding houses, the purple flowers on the corner of the street with the red fence—was the same as what she saw when she walked on this path. One day, these things may change. The purple flowers may get swapped for red ones. The red fence may get painted white. Someone may completely remodel their house. I may move, leaving this neighborhood, this path she took.

But right now, I can still see the same things she once saw on this path. I may not know what went through her mind when she looked at this view, but I am here where she once was.

When my mother became too sick to walk around the park, she would sit on the white patio chairs in front of the entrance of our house. I would find her sitting there when I returned from work staring at the park, people exercising, and families walking together. I would sit and join her, not saying anything. Instead of looking straight ahead, I would look at her, trying to remember every detail about her and that moment. She rarely said anything to me during these times. She just stared straight ahead. I'm not sure what my mother thought as she looked at the people who passed by our house. Did she wish she could join them? Or did she accept her condition by then? I will never know because I never asked. She was too lost in thought, and I didn't want to disturb her. I just wanted to sit next to her, remembering how alive she was next to me.

Now that she is no longer here, I sit where she once sat and stare at the same view she used to. This is the closest I can get to my mom now, being where she was, seeing what she saw. This is my comfort, knowing I can experience what she once did, knowing that she was once alive.

Even though I still think about all the missed opportunities with my mother, I will be forever grateful for all the ways my park brought my mother and me together. The future I want and the past I had will always be here within me in every step I take. I will learn how to walk with them, with my arms swinging robustly, exactly how my mother wanted.

CHAPTER 2

MAKE SURE YOU UPLOAD YOUR PHOTOS

———

I don't like crying. Once I start, I can't seem to stop. Not only does water pour from my eyes but my nose as well. I need an entire box of tissues to stop the gushing waterworks, but usually I am lucky if I manage to find one tissue. The worst is when this happens during a conversation I can't get out of. The more patiently people wait for me to stop so we can resume our discussion, the more I can't stop my tears.

I don't feel any better once I stop crying. My eyes are swollen and heavy, and they feel as if they will fall out of their sockets. A throbbing headache starts to form which can sometimes turn into a full-blown migraine if I don't take Tylenol in time. *Crying is exhausting.*

Thankfully, I don't cry that often.

And when my mother passed away, I learned to cry less.

I was especially determined to refrain from crying at my mother's funeral because I didn't want to distract the audience. I didn't want the tears and the sobbing to get in the way of what I wanted to share about my mother. In the week before her funeral, when relatives from out of town arrived, I used that time to practice holding back my tears. I learned that most of the time I don't have the urge to cry until I see another person's face. Once I see their expression, I feel everything they are feeling, their sadness and pity for me, except more intensely. I noticed that if I acknowledge their presence quickly enough with a nod and a look, I can avoid absorbing their emotions into mine.

That trick helped me through my eulogy and the entire funeral. I did not shed a single tear that day. I thought once the funeral was over, I could finally cry to my heart's content without worrying that I couldn't stop. However, after the funeral, the faucet for my tears didn't seem to work as well anymore.

As a night owl, I always enjoyed being the only one in my house awake late at night. With everyone in the house sleeping, it felt like I was the only one awake in the world, almost as if I had a secret time to myself. With my mother gone, the solitude I enjoyed turned into loneliness. It was only enjoyable when it was temporary—not permanent. In the weeks after my mother's funeral, I would wake up in the middle of the night and no longer be comforted by the solitude. The urge to cry for my mother's absence would come but the tears wouldn't. Disciplining myself not to cry really paid off since it was now difficult to cry even in these secret pockets of time.

I naively thought that this meant I could control my grief, that I could store grief away, the same way my mother stored away all our old photos in a container that sat on her closet floor. I would keep my grief in a box locked up under my bed. I would push the box all the way to the wall so that I could only reach it if I crawled under my bed with a flashlight in hand. It had to be somewhere hard to reach, out of sight so that I didn't need to think about it. Only when I was ready and no one was around could I take it out and examine my grief, one by one like the old photos I would stumble upon in my mother's container.

Wouldn't this be a nice way to store grief? How wonderful would it be if we could decide when and where we want to pull grief out from the hidden places.

Unfortunately, grief can't be tucked away so neatly and easily. There is too much of it to be contained. If you try to keep it locked up, it will eventually spill over. I learned this lesson in the most unexpected places, while I was sitting on a bleacher watching a high school graduation.

In my city, all the public high schools share the same football stadium for graduation. Even though I graduated from there in 2010, I continued to return to celebrate the graduations of my friends, younger cousins, and eventually the youth that I would teach in my Sunday School class.

It is always strange returning to the same place that was the first major turning point of a person's life. The football stadium feels like a place where time repeats itself over and over again as high school students go through the same routine to celebrate their crossover to adulthood. Even though the people here are different, the same anticipation, fears, and hopes for the future remain in the current graduates and their loved ones as it once did in their predecessors.

My graduation was no different than any other high school student's today. The same routine follows: get through the ceremony, find your family in the chaos of people looking for their graduate who is wearing the same colored gown as everyone else, take pictures with your family, try and find your friends in the same chaos of people before the security guard kicks you out for the next graduation. And then, you hope that your family didn't leave without you.

When I was in high school, I was so determined to take pictures with friends before we left for college. My mother was always going to be around, but I wasn't so sure about my friends and how college could change our friendships. I wanted to have proof, something to look back on when I felt nostalgic. I didn't know at that time that family members were not necessarily guaranteed to be around forever too.

When I look at the photos from my high school graduation with my family, I am reminded of how much I took my mother for granted. In the photos, I am standing with my mother, grandmother, and my younger cousins. We should be smiling but instead we are squinting at the camera. A few more shots and a different angle was all we needed for everyone to be more ready to smile for this momentous occasion. However, we didn't get a chance since I wanted to quickly look for my friends. My mother and I didn't even get a photo with each other. Looking back, I thought of how many pictures my mother took of me when I was younger. It is not surprising that I was in at least 70 percent of the photos in the albums my mother kept, seeing as I'm an only child. How long must my mother have waited for her only child to graduate from high school? The least I could have given her was a few more minutes to take a couple more pictures. Now that my mother is gone, I find myself thinking about all these spare minutes I could have given her and whether they could have made a difference in her happiness. These are the ordinary few minutes I wish we could have back, or that I could at least apologize for.

Seven years after my graduation, I would come back with my mother to the same place. This time I would snap a photo of my cousin and my mother. Every time I look at their photo, I can't help but feel envy and regret all at once. This was how my graduation photo was supposed to turn out. This was what I should have wanted, what I wish I had now.

Two years after my cousin graduated, I would return here once again to attend another graduation for one of my Sunday School students. As usual, the graduates looked tiny and far away in the center of the football stadium. While I waited for the ceremony to end, I used the time to finish sewing my graduation lei. As I threaded the ribbon together for the lei, I half listened to the conversations of neighboring families and the chatter of my friends next to me. I even heard the same occasional groan or cheer from people who were paying attention to the NBA finals. In the past few years, the Warriors would make it to the finals and a game almost always happened during graduation. Someone was always tracking the game.

Everything continued as it normally did. It was hard to separate the past from the present in a place where the only difference is the people and the time in between. All the years would blend into one if it wasn't for the Instagram posts documenting which year belonged to whom.

The only difference that year was that my mother had died two months ago. I tried not to think about my own high school graduation memories that were tied to this place. This was not the time to remember the past and all the regrets I had. This was the time to celebrate my friend's first big milestone. I would not let the disappointment I had for my younger self distract me, so I kept threading the ribbon together, focusing on finishing the lei in time to give it to my friend. Once I finished, I put the ribbon in my bag and decided to check my phone for any missed texts or the Warriors' score.

Strange, I thought to myself. My phone wasn't in my bag. I immediately checked the pockets in my jacket. *Nope, not there.* I stood up to see if I had left my phone where I was sitting.

"What's wrong?" my friend asked.

"I can't find my phone. Do you see it?" I asked.

As she was looking around her, I checked my back jean pockets. No luck again.

"Maybe you left it in the car?" she suggested.

"No, I remember using it earlier," I said with a sigh. This was bound to happen, as I am constantly misplacing my phone. Not wanting to look anymore, I started accepting that I lost my phone and thinking about how I was going to replace it. My phone was about three to four years old. It was about time I got a new one. It wasn't the end of the world.

…Until I realized that my phone contained photos of my mother from the last three to four years of her life. The most recent pictures were ones I did not want to remember. They were mainly reminders of how sick she was at the end, of what took her away.

But the earlier photos were her most healthy years, her happiest years, and her most free years. Those were the years between the first and second time she got cancer. It was when she realized that she should start enjoying the life that God gave her. There were photos from when we went to Santa Barbara for a vacation and San Diego for a family wedding and all the moments in between. These were the moments that I thought would continue. I didn't know that these photos would be the last reminders that my family wasn't always living in the uncertainty and disappointments that sickness would bring. These memories were the ones that were almost forgotten because they were overshadowed by her last year, the hardest and most painful. These were the ones that reminded me that life for my mother wasn't always like this, that those last days were not an accurate representation of her life. They were the needed reminders of who she really was, not the person she became when she got sick and depressed and died.

And I didn't store them in the cloud or on my computer. They only existed on my phone. I had been meaning to upload my pictures to another location, but I never found the time.

This is so like me, to put something off until it's too late. What if I never see the photos from how happy my mother was during those last few years? Will I only remember how sick she was?

I started becoming frantic at the thought of losing proof of my mother's most precious years. I wanted to search the entire stand for my phone, but the ceremony wasn't over yet. All I could do was sit with my thoughts, thinking about how clumsy and careless I was to lose my phone and not save my photos in another location.

The tears that I thought I could not cry anymore found their way back to me. Slowly and surely, they rolled down my face. Thankfully, they didn't come in waterfalls, just a slow quiet trickle with a few sniffles here and there.

A couple that sat in front of me noticed the tears and asked if I was alright.

I just nodded. There was not much to say. They looked concerned, unsure of what to do, and hesitantly turned around. My friends assured me that we would find my phone and that the ceremony would end soon.

I nodded again, afraid that if I said something, more tears would come. I thought I lost my mother when she passed away. I didn't know there were more ways I would continue to lose her. I wanted to go home and cry a pool of tears so I could sink into my sadness; I couldn't though, because I needed to find my phone. I needed to find my mother.

I couldn't stand how public my grief was at that moment, how unfair that grief could come and go when it wants, like an uninvited guest that expects you to be happy to see them. I wish I could save pockets of time for these visits from grief— carve out the moments for when and where and how I want to mourn, just pencil in my sadness on the calendar and compartmentalize all my emotions into neat little Marie Kondo boxes. But unlike the clothes I don't wear in my closet, emotions that don't spark joy just can't be thrown away. Instead, you sit and wait until grief is finished reminding you of what you lost. Eventually the tears stopped.

The graduates finally threw their caps in the air, and all their family and friends swarmed toward the field, leaving their seats. Once the bleachers were empty, my friends who were sitting with me and I began our long-awaited search. I was looking but not looking. My eyes were scanning the area frantically, but my mind was stuck on the possibility of leaving the stadium without my phone, without the pieces of my mother I could not let go.

My phone was so small and slim, and it was getting darker. What if we couldn't find it before it was time to leave? If the security guards start telling us to leave, maybe I could start crying again, and they will let us stay.

Or worse, what if someone actually took my phone, and I never get it back no matter how long we look for it? It was so outdated and scratched up. Why would anyone bother taking it? Didn't they know they didn't just steal a phone but my mother as well? Those kidnappers.

As I was occupied with thinking of different scenarios, two people from my church joined the search party. With their help, we were able to expand our search, and eventually one of them found my phone near the last step of the bleachers. Somehow it slid safely down to the bottom from where I sat at the top. When he handed me my phone, he said, "Make sure you upload your photos." It wasn't a suggestion, but a command.

When I held my phone in my hands, I felt as if I was given some part of my mother's life back. These files on my phone weren't her, but I would settle for them. These photos are the documentation and proof that my mother was once alive, and I want to keep them for as long as I can. I was so certain I was going to be punished for my carelessness, but instead I received a miracle.

Today, we take for granted how many photos we can snap in an instant. We can take as many photos as we want and delete the ones we don't like. When we had film cameras, you had to hope for the best with the limited number on each roll of film. You may have intended to take a photo of your family standing in front of the Christmas tree, but what you got a week later was a photo of half of your thumb with the Christmas tree peeking out from behind. Like the roll of film, I am trying to learn to accept the limited photos I have of my mother. These are all the photos I have left. That's it. There are no more chances to spend time with her, go places with her, take photos with her. There are no more new memories to make, only old memories to keep and preserve. This is all the time I had with her. Every day, I must confront this limit until I can learn to accept it.

Regret still runs deep when I look at the photos from my high school graduation or see others post current photos with their mothers. It's hard not to feel jealous when you are reminded of the limits you have reached. I thought I could ignore these regrets, bury them deep in my heart and try not to think about them. But it's exhausting pretending to do something that is not possible. When a person you love dies, there will always be something you should have done. This is the result of being imperfect people.

Whether it was naivety or arrogance to believe I could control grief, almost losing my phone showed me that I never had control. However, that doesn't mean that grief can control me. Learning how to live with grief in my heart is going to be a long process. At least I have made it past the first step: recognizing that its residence is permanent rather than temporary. I can no longer avoid the discomfort of mourning a loss or wait for it to one day leave, because it is not going anywhere. It will return time after time to remind me of all the places where my mother is now gone.

Sometimes, it feels unfair that when I look at photographs of my mother, I have to face the pain of loss. It is hard to look at what once was, to remember how things used to be and how they are not anymore. Every time I look at photos of my mother, I feel way too much for a 4" by 6" glossy paper. Am I happy that I can see her still frozen in time? Or am I sad that I can only see her in those still frames? It's always both.

Her photos look different now that she is gone, not because they've changed, but because I have. I don't see a younger version of my mother when I look at the photos; I see me longing for her, for the day when we are reunited. It is in these places of longing that I find hope because it reminds me that heaven will come soon enough. She was never meant to live forever on Earth. Time here is temporary. And one day we will be reunited with God and each other.

In the meantime, as I wait for heaven on Earth, I will look at these photographs of her and try not to ignore the painful regrets that may come with some memories. Instead of stifling those emotions, I will let them run their course, and I will remember to find hope afterwards.

There is one particular photo of her that I really like, a picture I took of her at the beach. She is standing right in the center of the frame with her back to the camera. She is wearing a light blue dress that matches the waters and the skies. There is something on the dress that makes it gleam when sunlight hits the water. To protect her skin from tanning, she is wearing her favorite sun hat with a brown polka dotted ribbon tied around it. The ends of the ribbon fall neatly down the back of her hat. Both her hands are raised high to the sky. At the time, I thought it was such a cheesy pose. Now when I see this photo, I see how alive she looks, how strong she stands, and how ready she is for tomorrow. I finally see what I needed all along in my grief: Hope. I am reminded that she's free where she is now—that this fleeting moment I captured on the beach depicts a joy and freedom I know she's found on the other side.

This is the hope I will carry with my grief.

CHAPTER 3

IT'S OKAY TO BE OKAY

One of my favorite things to do is watch Korean dramas. When I was in high school, Korean dramas were less diverse, often mainly romantic comedies that involved the dramatic love lines of characters who most often had no romantic experience. It was so fun to watch how these characters ended up together through the crazy plot devices thrown at them. Since then, Korean dramas have expanded to include more action-driven plots, dark, heavier themes, and slice-of-life healing stories. It is usually in these less popular, slower pace genres that I find pieces of my own life.

When I first came across the drama *Just Between Lovers*, I immediately fell in love with the story of how two broken characters find healing in each other from their shared experience of a tragedy in their childhood. What happened to them was so dramatic, yet the story unfolds gently and softly. Now that I have a better understanding of grief, I've come to appreciate the characters much more than before.

Just Between Lovers is about two people, Moon Soo and Gang Doo, who first meet as young teenagers trapped under the debris of a mall. Years later, they meet again when they are picked to work on a project to honor the anniversary of the collapse of the mall. In the tragedy, Moon Soo loses her younger sister, and her parents' marriage comes undone. Her mother eventually becomes an alcoholic due to the grief of losing her younger daughter. Most of the time, Moon Soo is a dutiful daughter, often absorbing all the harsh comments her mother says out of grief. Gang Doo loses his father and his dream of playing soccer from the injury that resulted from the incident. From then, he faces hardship after hardship, taking on his late mother's medical bill debt, trying to pay for his sister's medical school tuition, and dealing with the psychological trauma of the collapse. It is not surprising that we find him years later rough around the edges and angry at the world.

In episode thirteen, Moon Soo wakes up in the room of her friend's house after having an awful fight with her mother. She discovers that Gang Doo is outside waiting for her. In this tender moment, Gang Doo comforts her about the fight she had earlier. She is thankful for his care and says, "I like you so much that I wonder if it's okay for me to feel this way."

He says, "It's okay. You have to. If it weren't for that accident, I'm sure everything would have been perfect."

Suddenly, the scene switches to the mall when it collapsed. The scene is played backward, as if reversing time to right before the collapse when the two teenagers were in the mall. They never meet. The next scenes show their "reimagined" futures. He is a star soccer player. She is watching the game on her phone, very happy and carefree. Other characters show up in the future as well. One couple is watching the game, and they are cheering for him and smile lovingly at each other. Like Moon Soo's parents, this couple's relationship was severely impacted by the accident, but here in this future, their relationship continues strongly.

When I first watched this drama in 2017, the "reimagined" future scene stuck with me for a very long time. It was bittersweet to watch how happy the characters were in the rewritten timeline. It felt as if the director wanted to give an homage to the characters' dreams from their youth by showing the future they hoped for.

This scene hits differently after my mom died.

Before, I saw my life in one straight, linear timeline. When my mother passed away, the timeline broke into two pieces—everything before she died and everything that came afterwards.

My life continues in that second piece of the broken timeline, inching forward as it creates my past, present, and future. As I continue onward, I can't help but think of another timeline that runs parallel to the one I am on. When something happens in my life, whether major or minor, joyful or sorrowful, good or bad, I instinctively imagine the other timeline where my mother is still alive. Sometimes, when I consider both timelines side by side, it feels as though I was given a choice and picked the wrong one. But the truth is, I was never given a choice. If I could choose, I would have never picked this timeline. As much as I try to ignore this parallel, imaginary timeline, it continues to exist and persist in how I see my life unfold, reminding me of what could have been, another version of my life I so wish I could have.

After my mother died, I realized the "reimagined" future in the drama wasn't merely a nice interlude for the viewers to see what life could have been if the big accident didn't happen. This was the future that haunts the characters, flowing next to their current life, reminding them of all the things they lost in the accident.

My imagined future with my mother doesn't just show up in the major events; it runs through the ordinary mundane moments as well.

When my mother was alive, we never celebrated her birthday, and I never thought much about it because birthdays weren't considered a special occasion in our household. We never celebrated my grandmother's birthday either because hers happened around the same time my grandfather died. My parents were more celebratory of my birthday when I was young and cute, but when I became an adult, we had a new tradition. When I started driving, my mother told me to buy my own birthday cake for dinner. Sometimes, my friends or family would drop gifts off at our house for me. My mother would take a picture of me with my cake and the gifts people gave me and post on WeChat, a Chinese social media platform. She really made it seem as if we put in some effort to celebrate my birthday. But I didn't mind; the less pressure to celebrate, the happier I was. Our tradition was simple and sweet, just the way I like it.

When she died, my dad wanted to find her real birthday to put on the gravestone. In America, my mother didn't use the exact date of her birth from the traditional Chinese calendar. It had been so long since anyone had celebrated her real birthday that it took a while for my aunt and grandmother to confirm what the actual date was. After some time, they discovered that her birthday was on September 29th. In 2020, we decided to celebrate her birthday for the very first time.

(If your loved ones are still alive, I would recommend celebrating their birthday before they die—at least once would be nice.)

My mother's first birthday celebration after her passing was on a very busy day for me. In the weeks leading to her birthday, I was in charge of transitioning the nonprofit that I worked at to go remote indefinitely due to COVID-19. Rather than paying for rent, we decided it would be better to pay for a public storage unit to hold all our furniture and supplies as we waited for the pandemic to end. The last and final part of this project was to move all the agency's belongings to the public storage unit, which was scheduled on the same day as my mother's birthday.

I could not believe that my mother's birthday was going to happen on the same day as the culmination of everything I was preparing for. I was anticipating a very hectic, stressful, and tiring day. Not only did I come home late the night before, but I had to get up especially early to visit my mother on the other side of the Bay. Thankfully, my boss was able to meet the movers first thing in the morning, but I felt unsettled not being there when they came.

Ignoring my restlessness the next day, I tried to focus on remembering my mother. At her grave site, it was cold and windy, just the way I liked it. Unlike people with seasonal affective disorder, gloomy weather makes me happy because I feel refreshed from the chilliness. After my sleepiness wore off, I realized that visiting my mother at the cemetery was not a bad way to start the day. It was like visiting a park, only quieter. This was also the first time my grandmother left the house in months. Because of her age, we were being very cautious during the pandemic. It was nice to see her walk around the memorial park.

Strangely, I didn't feel especially sad going to the memorial site. It is simply where my mother is buried. I have no memories of the place attached to my mother since this was where she came after she died. If anything, I feel really relaxed when I go to the cemetery because of how peaceful, quiet, and beautiful the park is. If we are lucky, we get to see deer meandering around the park.

We don't usually stay for too long—thirty minutes at the most. I was able make it back to the office while it was still considered morning. By the time I made it there to relieve my boss of her duty, I was pleasantly surprised to see that the movers had already moved a majority of the furniture and supplies into the truck. Once we arrived at the public storage, they quickly moved all the items into the unit, and I was given the rest of the day off.

Unsure of what to do, I called my best friend who lived nearby and asked if she wanted to get lunch. She suggested I pick up poke, one of my favorite meals, on the way to her house. Eating in the comfort of her home while chatting aimlessly was incredibly relaxing after the busy morning. As I was heading home, I realized that it was National Coffee Day. As a coffee lover, the timeliness of this day could not have made me happier. Naturally, I had to drop by my favorite coffee shop to pick up an iced oat latte.

At the end of the day, I started to replay all the things that happened to me, something I hadn't done in a while because of how busy my days were. In my focus on getting from point A to B in my schedule, I forgot that happiness wasn't that hard to find. It was there all along, wrapped up in the foggy morning at my mother's grave, the gate going down on my month-long finished project, the unplanned lunch with my dear friend, an iced oat latte, and trust that God would get me through every single task.

As I started to let myself sink fully into the joys of those small victories, something held me back from fully appreciating my accomplishments that day. This was such an unexpected, good day with a balance of productivity, good friends, coffee, and well-deserved rest. It was supposed to make me feel fulfilled and satisfied; instead, grief came back and reminded me of how incomplete that day was. Because as good as that day was, it couldn't have been perfect. My mother was still gone.

Even though visiting her in the morning didn't weigh my day down or make me feel especially sad; her absence was still there. Just like the small victories, grief shows up in these small cracks of an almost perfect day. Sometimes, grief can hurt very painfully in the most unexpected places, but sometimes it feels like paper cuts, reminding you that you are not fully healed, that there are still small places in you that hurt.

Before, all my good days were simply good days. There was nothing to mull over or remember, nothing holding me back from appreciating the day. Now when I have good days, I can't help but ask myself, *But, did you have a really good day? Can days truly be good without your mother?* Similar to Moon Soo, I wonder if it is okay for me to feel this way—to feel happy when my mother is gone.

When I think of everything good that happens to me, I am always reminded afterwards of how I can't share this news with my mother. Grief disrupted my timeline and marked all the days after as incomplete, no matter how great they were.

When I think back to how Gang Doo said, "If it weren't for that accident, I'm sure everything would have been perfect," I think he may have been wrong. Since everything that happened to him after the mall collapse was so unfortunate, he naturally believes that if the accident didn't happen, everything would have gone right in his life. The truth is he doesn't know. No one knows. Perhaps, he could have still injured his leg another way and still lost his chance to play soccer professionally. The future is full of unknowns, but what is certain is that everyone will face grief.

Eventually, the people we love will die. The older we become, the more we will see how much suffering exists in the world, how much evil there is out there and in us. There was never a guarantee that, if my mother didn't die, I would have had a perfect life, escaping grief and pain. I definitely wish I didn't have to experience it firsthand with my mother's death, but I would have faced suffering and sorrow eventually, one way or another.

Grief reminds me of how incomplete and imperfect the world truly is because of all the suffering and brokenness that continues to exist in humanity. Now I can see more clearly how my days were never perfect to begin with; there will always be something wrong when pain prevails so strongly in the world.

Rather than lean into the incomplete aftertaste of grief, I am learning how to find hope there instead of sorrow and hopelessness. My mother believed that this world wouldn't be incomplete forever. Eternity will come, and those days will be completely, wholly perfect. This is the hope I cling to when I am reminded of my loss on good days: that my grief won't last forever.

In the meantime, as I wait for eternity to come, I will try to find the bittersweet spot between remembering my grief and embracing happiness. Even though it is still hard to fully embrace all the happiness that comes my way with my loss, I don't want to resist all of the joys and victories that I will come across either.

After, the "reimagined" future scene is over, the story switches back to our two main characters. Gang Doo takes Moon Soo's hand and says, "So we have to work hard. We have to be happier than anyone out there."

Gang Doo is telling Moon Soo what she needs to hear; it's okay for her to be happy, even if it's a battle to acknowledge and accept because of her guilt and grief. So many times, we have to begrudgingly accept that it's okay to not be okay, to accept that we are human and not perfect. In grief, there is the opposite struggle. In the moments when you realize that you're okay, you start to resist it because you remember why you weren't okay to begin with. These are the ordinary moments where the labor of grief comes in, where you have to work hard to remind yourself that it's okay to be okay. And if you've managed to fight those stubborn feelings off and accept how good a day was—how you're doing just fine—you have to do it all over again. It's not one big battle but many small ones throughout your life.

Grief does make it harder, but not impossible, to accept happiness. Some days, I can happily accept the big accomplishments, small victories, and good things that come my way. Other times, when the incomplete aftertaste lingers too long after a good thing, I will try my best to lean into hope. On those days, I will remind myself that even though my days feel so incomplete without my mother, I will never stop waiting to be filled to the top.

CHAPTER 4

GO WITH THE CURRENTS

———

I'm not a brave or adventurous person. I don't like driving and am afraid of flying, so I rarely travel outside of California or internationally. If I do drive, I prefer to keep within a fifteen-mile radius of my house. I would rather watch YouTube vlogs or my friend's Instagram stories about their travels than travel myself. I don't feel envious but excited that I can get a glimpse of the world from the comfort of my home. Traveling has always been more of a burden than a reward.

If there's one thing people know about me, it is that I am deathly afraid of birds. This alone explains why I prefer to stay home and why leaving my house stresses me out. In case you didn't know, birds are everywhere. They hide under cars, visit the park next to my house, frequent the streets of Chinatown as much as Asian grandparents, and are always waiting for me outside the BART station. The world is a very terrifying place when you have a bird phobia.

My world is smaller than others, especially compared to my millennial peers who enjoy exploring every corner of the world, pushing their boundaries as far as they can. Their Instagram feeds are filled with food adventures and travel escapades from everywhere and anywhere. Mine is filled with multiple posts of the same drink from the same café—iced oat latte in the summer, drip coffee with a splash of oat milk in the winter. And if I am feeling adventurous, I will get the seasonal drink.

It is not surprising that my friends are creatures of habits. For a few years after college, our routine was to meet at my favorite coffee shop in my town to study or work, chat occasionally in between, then eat at the Mediterranean place ten minutes away. Not wanting to go home yet, we would often waste time nearby at the Whole Foods market. Rather than look for groceries, we played a game of who could find the most unnecessarily expensive and healthy item. We have repeated this routine so many times that it's become infamous among my circle of friends. Even the conversation rarely changes. Once, my friend made a comment that if he missed a hangout, he knew he wasn't missing much. This wasn't meant as an insult, but a fact.

If we wanted to change things up, we would switch this routine to go to our favorite matcha soft serve spot: Somisomi. This was how the "forty-year plan" was born, a reference to the Israelites wandering the desert for forty years. The "desert" in our case was the soft serve ice cream. We are really not as clever or funny as we like to believe. But these are my friends, these are my people that I am wandering the desert with, and this is where I belong. Clearly, I don't like change. I like predictability and routine. No surprises for me. Like still waters, I want everything to stay the same and to avoid the waves as much as I can.

When change did happen, it merely involved adjusting to a different scenario. For most of my life, the big crucial changes happened at these turning points of transitioning to a new environment. In fourth grade, I moved from Texas back to California. To my young self, that was the most life-altering event I had experienced. Even though I was born in California, Texas was all I had known. Moving back to the West Coast meant leaving my friends and living in a place I could hardly remember. To an elementary school–aged kid, it was all very scary and dramatic, but Texas soon became a place in the past once I made friends.

Even though I never made that far of a move ever again, I did make my way to new environments in the natural course of adjusting to a new campus in middle school, high school, and college. I still wasn't a huge fan of these transitions, especially the last one. While my peers looked forward to the thrills of leaving home, I was thinking about how much I would miss having my parents around and the solitude of having my own room.

Despite getting homesick easily, I knew I would eventually adjust to college life. It would just take some time. In that way, change was predictable because I knew after the growing pains, I would be comfortable again once I became familiar with my new surroundings. The environment would be different, but I could count on myself being the same.

When my mother died, the opposite happened. Everything around me stayed the same. My friends continued to meet at our usual coffee shop every month. My church had the same people and the same ongoing ministries and activities. My job was still there, waiting for me to return. I was still living in the same city, the same house, the same room. Everything was in exactly the right place. Nothing had moved or changed in my environment. Nothing was out of place.

Except my mother was gone. I was the thing that was different this time. This was truly the most life-altering change in my entire life, not moving back to California. There was no way I could be the same person anymore. I was now someone without a mother, someone whose mother was no longer alive. Death is now part of me wherever I go, reminding me how much my mother is gone, how incomplete I will always be. The world was the same, but my world was different.

Like how I've constantly resisted change, I continued to cling onto the familiarity of my surroundings. Usually in movies or stories, when someone has experienced such a traumatic change, they will do something drastic, like cutting off their hair or moving across the country. Unable to confront their grief, they make changes to what they can control. For me, I found my control in keeping everything as it was. I wanted to seamlessly go back to how things were before, even if it hurt to be reminded of my mother's absence in those places. When my mother's cancer returned, our lives suddenly became so unstable and turbulent. We didn't know whether her treatment would work, which clinical trial would accept her, what her test results would be, and how much longer she would have to live. I was so tired of how uncertain the future was. I didn't know if I had become exhausted from hoping she wouldn't die or from waiting for her to die. It all felt the same at the end.

After a week of bereavement and three weeks of paid time off, I was ready to settle back to the way things were, as if my mother never had cancer and left us. It wasn't that hard to slip back to the same routine, the same habits, the same people and places. There were no new faces, no new projects or activities, nothing I wanted to explore or try. I would keep everything the same for as long as I could to make up for the biggest traumatic change in my life.

I kept sticking to the same routine, day after day, until the summertime where I got roped into volunteering to coordinate games for my church's annual summer retreat. This was the only time all the sister churches gathered. Despite going to my church for years, I had never gone to a summer retreat when I was younger since my parents worked all the time.

I often forgot that my church was part of a network of churches, despite the fact that our church name had a number in it to signify our connection to these series of churches. For the retreat, I was paired with two people, each from a different sister church in completely different parts of the Bay Area. Truth be told, I wasn't planning on making friends; I just wanted to plan the games well. I did not expect our weekly meetings to go on until 2 or 3 a.m. This would have been fine if we were in college, but we were working adults. We really could have finished the meetings by midnight, but random conversations kept us going past the appropriate time to finish.

My mother would have been appalled at how late we stayed up. Regardless of whether I was in high school or an adult, my mother would check on me in the middle of the night. When she discovered that I was still awake, she would yell, "Why are you still up? Your organs need to be asleep right now for them to function well!"

I will admit it was probably a poor decision to not put the tangent topics in parking lots for another time, but I never regretted staying up late. After college, I rarely made new friends, let alone people my age. For the first time in a long time, I finally met people that I clicked instantly with. It was a welcome change, a little something different that I could enjoy. Everything was going well until one of my friends asked if we wanted to go river rafting with the young adults from his church.

I never understood why people did things like river rafting. It looked dangerous and wet.

I was suddenly reminded of how new this friendship was, how much they didn't know me. This was something a brave and adventurous person would do—trying a new activity with a group of people that they barely knew. Going to an event where you didn't know anyone was intimidating but doable if you knew the event would end after a few hours. River rafting was going to take an entire day. Most of the time, when I venture to a new place or try a new activity, it is because a friend asked me to join them. I don't go to experience the activity, the place, or the food; I go because I want to spend time with the people that asked me to. If I didn't have any friends, I would stay home all day long, maybe occasionally going to coffee shops, thrift stores, or bookstores. Those places would be enough for me but because I love my friends and family, I resist my homebody tendencies.

Since I didn't know the people who would be going well, I figured it wouldn't be hard to opt out of this adventure. Before I could respond, my other friend messaged me and used the oldest trick in the book, the "I'll go if you go" con. Suddenly, my choice wasn't entirely about me anymore. I didn't want her to not go because of me. We would also be going into this group together as newcomers, which made the event less intimidating. My decision to not go suddenly shifted as I debated what I should do. In this internal debate, I started to examine why I was so set on not going, why I was so afraid of trying new things and meeting new people. My natural-self mode may be a slothful homebody, but I usually wasn't this resistant, oftentimes easily swayed if I really liked the people.

As I dived into the grottoes of my mind, I discovered that I was unusually fixated on river rafting as a new activity that I didn't want to try. Rationally, I knew that river rafting was not going to change anything about myself, but I couldn't help but feel it was going to be a catalyst for something I couldn't control. In the grand scheme of things, going river rafting was a very micro decision. But these small decisions tend to lead to bigger ones, which will eventually snowball into many small decisions that will make up a different version of myself. What was so troubling about this water activity was not the risk of drowning but that it was something I had never done before when my mother was alive.

I didn't want to become a person who went river rafting. This would be something my mother wouldn't know about me. Even though I know she wasn't coming back, I didn't want to become someone my mother wouldn't recognize from these micro changes. This was how I could still keep a part of her with me—by staying as I was. I have always been afraid of change, but this time it meant moving further away from the version of myself that my mother knew. If she couldn't change, I wouldn't either. If I tried river rafting, what other things would I want to try? What other ways would I start to evolve? What other versions of myself would my mother never be aware of?

This was how I wanted to hold onto my grief.

Yet, the moment I realized how much I wanted to keep myself from changing was also the moment that I realized I couldn't continue this way. It was unrealistic to believe that I could stay the same forever. I would have to face these changes coming my way by taking the necessary steps.

River rafting was no longer something that I didn't want to do but needed to do. It was time to push myself over this threshold that I created to keep my grief from hurting me so deeply. I needed to see if I could face the changes ahead. If I couldn't agree to try this new activity with people I just met, how was I going to navigate through life when more unexpected and intensive things happen?

It turned out to be a really great decision. Though I was right about river rafting; it was very wet.

Despite the countless times I was so sure I was going to get thrown off the boat, I never did. For a first-timer, the currents felt aggressive, but instead of finding fear in these turbulent moments like I anticipated, I found excitement. Before going river rafting, I was so ready to be afraid and uncomfortable. I didn't know I could have fun.

I had expected to be paddling through the rough currents the entire time, but there were a lot of moments to rest in between. There were times when all we did was wait in stillness right before the sudden shift to water picking up and gushing fiercely onward. I thought our little raft would be at the mercy of the flow of the water, rushing us from one place to the next, carrying us on a whim wherever it wanted us to go. I didn't know that the river was capable of being gentle, nudging us slowly forward at times. If the scenery didn't change before me, I would have thought our raft remained still. As we slowly inched ahead, I let myself sink into these moments where I could sit back and look at the view in front of me, full of trees that stretched tall toward the sky high above and the cool river promising adventure at the next turn. From soaking in this nature scene, I felt as if nothing could go wrong. All I had to do was be still and enjoy the presence of God in the world He created.

I came expecting a battle between me and the river; I didn't realize that I would be willing to surrender to the streams and that I could trust where it would take me. I always thought that surrendering meant giving up, which is why I fought so hard against the currents of time. I thought that if I could keep myself and everything around me from changing, then I could lessen the gap between who I was when my mother died and who I was becoming without her. I was afraid to confront the reality that my mother wasn't around to see these new experiences I was undergoing, no matter how minuscule. I thought by keeping these micro changes from happening, I could keep her close to me. I wanted some way to prevent time from separating us as we moved further and further away from each other with each day passing. I didn't know how else I could hold onto my mother.

I wanted to be unmoving and unyielding against time, like a rock firmly planted in the middle of a gushing river. But that was impossible, no matter how stubborn I was to be planted in the same spot. Nothing stays the same forever— not me or the world outside of me. To stay the same meant that people were perfect, that they don't need to grow or mature anymore because there wasn't any need for change. Only a perfect person could remain the same and constant. And I was far from perfect. I could not stay the same. There were still so many places in me that needed to be watered and that needed to grow. The waves are there for a reason—not simply to rock the boat but to mold me and change me into someone kinder, more compassionate and patient, and more loving. I am still unfinished, like a jar of clay that still needs to be sculpted before it can harden.

I wish I could say that after this epiphany of how I was handling my grief, I learned to stop resisting and to surrender completely. I was hoping that once I saw how much I was holding back, I could embrace the future easier and all the changes it would bring. If only grief was that easy. Instead, I need to continually remind myself that I can't keep holding onto the version of myself from when my mother was alive. Even though I know it is fruitless, I still want to keep resisting and fighting because of how much I want to go back to the way things were. These are the battles that are happening inside of me. This is what I do when I miss my mom; I mull over how every little or major decision will bring me further away from her.

But I think about how sad she would be if she knew how I was preventing myself from growing and letting new experiences change me for the better. My mother would not want this for me. If I told her I was going river rafting, she would first be worried about me drowning, but she wouldn't stop me. My mother would want me to try new experiences and make new friends. My mother's life stopped on April 29, 2019. Mine kept going and will continue for however long I am meant to be here. It is hard to not look back. The further I move from where her life stopped, the more I want to run back to it.

It is a never-ending battle full of losses and victories. Sometimes, I can't let go of how much I want to stay the same, and I find myself stubbornly swimming against the currents. I will never enjoy drifting away from who I was when my mother was alive. But the more I fight, the more I realize how hard it is to continue going upstream. I am learning to accept that the distance is going to keep growing; it will get longer and longer. I am trying to trust that where the river leads me is good, even if it flows to places that I don't feel ready for. There is no way I can stop moving. There is no way I can stop time.

CHAPTER 5

BEING AN ADULT ISN'T EASY

I thought that by the time I turned twenty-seven, I'd be getting married. Instead, my mother died.

When I was younger, I was so sure I was going to get married when I became an adult because that was one of the many things adults did: they went to college, found a job, started dating, got married, bought a house with a white picket fence, had 2.5 kids, and died. As a child, I never thought about how these things came to be or the possibility of them not happening. These were things that happened to everyone when they grew up.

I remember once when I was in Sunday School, my teacher asked the kids in my classroom what they wanted to be one day. A younger student shouted, "I want to be a mommy when I grow up." Like my Sunday School teacher, my mother laughed so hard when I shared the story with her.

Adults were always smiling and laughing when you told them what you wanted to be when you were younger. It's hard not to think anything is possible when you are a kid. All you had to do was use your imagination when you thought of the future. Anything was possible. It was always fun swapping daydreams with your friends about your future job and what your wedding would look like. We were like genies, conjuring up a world where everything was made of wishes. However, as I became older, these conversations became heavier with greater expectations as reality drew closer. The adults smiled and laughed less. They thought it was cute when you were five and wanted to be an artist; when you were fifteen, they asked you how much money artists earned.

Once I made it to college, I began to see that things don't just fall into place so easily. Just because I was accepted into my top school didn't mean I knew the right major for me or what career I should pursue. Despite my unclear future goals, I decided to put a timeline on my adult milestones so it seemed like I knew where my future was headed. I latched onto the idea of twenty-seven being the year where I would accomplish the major adult checkpoints: I would establish my career by then and get married too. I originally wanted to get married by twenty-five. These extra two years would be more than enough time for me to transform into a full-fledged adult. I thought I was being realistic, not imaginative.

Making plans is fun, but implementing them? Not so much. It's always easier said than done.

Growing up, my parents always talked highly about my Aunt Jenny, who went to the University of California, Davis for college, then medical school, and became a doctor. She was the pride of our family and every immigrant parent's dream come true. Hearing my parents talk about my aunt must have made me subconsciously want to go to UC Davis since I couldn't explain why it was my first choice. I did not know much about the school except it was where my aunt went, and it was only one and a half hours away from home.

Luckily, I was accepted into UC Davis, but once I got there, I finally realized that I didn't know why I was there or what I wanted to do. In high school, I had focused so much on getting into college that I didn't actually think about what career path I wanted to pursue. Going in undeclared couldn't have been more fitting.

The only thing that was clear to me was that I didn't want to major in hard sciences. After two years, I somehow landed on not one but two degrees: sociology and community and regional development. I naively thought that once I declared my major, the hard part of college was over. While my friends stressed over the future, their GPAs, and finding an internship, I was merely satisfied with declaring my majors. On one hand, my shortsightedness made college a lot less stressful than my peers, but on the other hand, I left college as clueless about what I wanted to be as when I first started. Unsure of where to go, I naturally found my way to the nonprofit world since a majority of my studies had focused on inequities and social stratification. In the meantime, my friends switched career paths, found jobs that had nothing to do with their majors, or went back to school. Despite being the one who put the least thought into her future, it turned out that most of my friends were just as unsure as I was about the future. After all their years searching and exploring, most of my friends now seem to have finally found the career or direction they were looking for.

I thought my postgrad years would be like everyone else's: feeling lost but attempting to find some direction. Instead, those years were marked by my mother's cancer. At one point, when her cancer was in remission, I started thinking more intentionally about what I wanted to do with my life, and I was even becoming open to the idea of using dating apps, too.

But then, my mother's cancer came back aggressively, and I was content with having a job I liked and was capable in. There were too many hospital visits, emergency room visits, and clinical trials to think about my future when my mother's was so uncertain. I didn't want to think about looking into graduate programs or applying for other jobs. I had had enough disappointments by then.

Even though I put a pause on thinking about my career, I didn't forget about how I wanted to get married at twenty-seven. This dream resurfaced in full force during the last six months of my mother's life. I didn't want to get married simply because I wanted to be with someone. Getting married wasn't just my dream as a kid; it was my mother's as well. I wanted her dream for us. I wanted to give her something to be happy about, something to celebrate as she was dying.

So, I clung to this idea toward the end. I thought the miracle would be that either I suddenly found someone to get married to or my mother would live far longer than we thought. I know it was unrealistic, but I wanted something to go right, to go according to plan when everything I had imagined for myself was so far from what I wanted.

It wasn't until I attended my friends' weddings that I confronted the reality of my mother's impending death, not once but twice in the same weekend.

I was really looking forward to seeing my friends get married. I couldn't wait to see all my college friends and celebrate these happy, joyful, blessed occasions together. Most of all, I wanted a break from my mother dying. Just for one weekend, I wanted to be a guest at a wedding, a friend someone hasn't seen in a long time, somebody whose mother wasn't dying. I wanted to be who I was before my mother's cancer. For a few moments, I wanted to remember what that was like. I was hesitant to leave my mother, but I wanted to be free for a weekend and regain a bit of my former life.

However, no matter how far I went, how much I pretended that my mother wasn't dying, grief had a way of creeping up on me in the most unexpected places and reminding me of my loss in the most vulnerable way. I thought I was fine when I chatted with my friends in the car, when I caught up with people I hadn't seen in a long time, and when I saw the beautiful bride walk down the aisle. As I watched the ceremony in front of me and listened to the personal anecdotes of how God brought two imperfect people together, I felt water on my face.

Strange. There was no way it could rain on this gorgeous sunny day. My nose started sniffling, which was odd because I don't have allergies. There was only one explanation: I was crying. Thankfully, I was crying quietly, and my friends and I were sitting in the back. Most of all, I was really thankful for the one napkin I had in my purse. I felt so awkward, so embarrassed holding back my sniffles and tears, afraid that someone thought I was crying because I was an overly sentimental person.

Was I that happy for my friend? Yes, but not to the point of tears.

Then I watched as my friend and her groom greeted their two sets of parents.

I finally realized that the dream I was clinging to was not going to happen. I was never going to see my mother at my wedding.

Whenever my friends and I would discuss our future weddings, we would talk about the kinds of dresses we wanted, what colors our bridesmaid dresses would be, and what season we wanted to get married in. Now, all those things seem trivial when the one thing I want the most for my wedding is impossible. My urgency for marriage wasn't just because I wanted to give my mother a bit of happiness. Once I knew she could never be at my wedding, I wanted her there even more desperately.

Two weeks later, my mother died.

My urgency for marriage and a family died on the same day my mother did.

If my mother were alive, I know exactly how she would respond to that statement. Exasperated, she would say, "Stop, don't say that!" Then she would turn around, and that would be the end of the conversation. This was the same response I received from her every single time I brought up the possibility of not getting married or having children. So strong was her fear of me not getting married that she wouldn't even want to talk about the possibility; she feared saying it out loud would make it come true.

But I can't imagine getting married without the person who wants to see it happen the most.

Before my mother passed away, I was watching a Korean drama called *Go Back Couple*, starring one of my favorite actresses, Jang Na-ra. In the drama, Jang Na-ra played a wife, Jin-joo Ma, who is in an unhappy marriage. The premise of the show is that she and her husband time travel back to their early twenties, when they met in college and fell in love. Still angry at each other, they relive their college days by attempting to avoid each other, trying not to fall for each other again.

In the first episode, Jin-joo is ecstatic to discover she is back in the past where her mother is still alive. Once she sees her mother for the first time, Jin-joo follows her around like a small child. Everywhere her mother goes—whether it's to the kitchen to cook or to the bathroom to clean—Jin-joo is following right behind her, never letting her out of sight. If I could travel back in time, I would want to be near my mother again, too, so that I could hold her hand, hear her voice calling my name again, and remember what she smelled like. All the little details I took for granted about my mother, they fade each and every day without her here to remind me of them. I wonder how many things I have already forgotten about her, how many more I will soon forget. How much more of her will I keep losing?

As much as she enjoys having her mother back, she also remembers how devastating her mother's absence will be. In episode eight, Jin-joo painfully remembers the birth of her son in the future. At the hospital, she sees her husband and her mother-in-law holding her child joyfully in their arms. Jin-joo watches them bitterly as she thinks about how her mother is not with her during what is supposed to be one of the happiest moments of her life.

Loss isn't just about mourning what you lost in the past, but also what you will not have in the future. Loss will find its way to all the future occasions that you thought were reserved only for celebration: birthdays, anniversaries, graduations, marriages. Before the person died, you could celebrate these happy events freely. Now they serve as reminders of how the person you loved continues to be missing from your life. Loss exists in all of the places that the person should be but can't be. It never stops, not even for the joyous moments.

Now when I think about these potential future milestones, I don't wait impatiently or yearn excitedly for them anymore. Instead, what I see in those places is my mother's absence. If I were to get married one day, I would have to confront my mother's death on my wedding day. And if I have children one day, will I look onward like Jin-joo, bitterly remembering what I lost in the face of my child who I will have gained that day?

I wish I could separate my sorrow from my joy in all these future events so that I could face them more easily. Instead, sorrow and joy are like two different colors that get mixed together. Once combined, they are impossible to pull apart. You have to make do with the new color.

This was not what I thought thinking of my wedding or future was going to be like.

When I was in high school, I was so curious about what I would be like as an adult. What kind of person would I date and get married to? What would my wedding be like? What kind of job would I have? How many children would I have? There were so many questions I had for the adult version of myself. I thought she was going to make it through the growing pains of adulthood and come out successful, confident, and married to someone who looked like a Korean idol while emulating the characteristics of Jesus. I clearly thought highly of future me. Most of all, I was hoping my future self would be braver, more sure of herself and what she wanted in life.

Instead, my mother died, and now at the age of twenty-seven, I am even more unsure of what I want than when I was in high school. Before, I was impatiently waiting for these things to fall into place, for me to reach the same milestones as my friends. Now, my mother's absence waits for me in those places.

When I used to daydream about my future wedding, I thought about what colors I wanted for the bridesmaid dresses, what kind of food I would serve, and what the theme would be. Now I think about all the fights my mother and I will not have. I would have wanted to find a sustainable or thrifted wedding dress that was simple so that I could re-wear it. My mother would have wanted something more traditional and extravagant and definitely not used. My wedding was supposed to be a tug of war between what I wanted and what she wanted. It was going to end with me wanting her approval and her wanting me to be happy. Now, my future wedding will not be made up of compromises but of decisions I made without her.

Before, I would daydream and wonder if my future husband would look like the Korean celebrities I like or if our story would be like the plots in a Korean drama. Now, I think about how my mother said she bought our minivan because she wanted to have enough room for her and my dad to travel with my future husband and children. I don't know if I am brave enough to do all the things she wanted for me without her.

My mother would be upset if she knew that her absence made me reevaluate all the things she wanted for me, all the things she hoped and prayed for.

In my youth, I wanted to grow up, get married, and have kids because that's what everyone did, and that's what my family wanted for me. With my mom around, I would have kept hoping for these things to happen. Without my mother, I am leaning into the side of me that I never paid attention to before. As an only child who has never dated, I am very protective about my own solitude. As much as I daydream about what it is like to be married, I know I will struggle to give up my alone time. Even though I love playing with my friends' kids, I don't know if I have the confidence to have my own and the energy to raise one.

Now that my mother is gone, the fuel for these things to happen is gone as well. I still believe that marriage and children are blessings, and I still believe that it would be nice to have them one day. However, I want to take my time getting there if these things are meant to happen for me. God will provide for me whether I am single or not. I will need Him either way.

In the last stretch of my mother's life, I was filled with rush and urgency for these things to happen, to squeeze in one last milestone before she died. Now that she is no longer here, my wish for her to be at my wedding can no longer be fulfilled. In this way, there is a bit of relief when wishes, dreams, and hopes die. Because now that you know what cannot happen, you are free to move on to other things. You are no longer tied down by things that weren't meant to happen.

All the things that I wanted to happen at twenty-seven didn't. The thing that I thought would never happen did.

Grief carved out this different path for me to take and made me realize that I was comparing the pace of my timeline too much with others. I am trying to not base my career accomplishments and dating life (or lack of dating life) on those around me. I want to go at my own pace, even if it looks slower to others. I don't want to rush into things I am not ready for. I certainly don't want people to see my mother's absence as an excuse to not pursue marriage and family. That is not an excuse; that is my grief creating a different path for me.

When I look at the grief that came into my life, I often feel like a plant that was suddenly moved to a different environment. Not used to this location, the stems are unable to find where the light once was. At first, this transition may seem as if it is causing too much stress for the plant. Sometimes, I can't help but feel that others will start to lose confidence on whether this plant can grow again. But if they give it some time, then they will see that the stem and leaves weren't shrinking back from where it once stood tall but arching towards a different direction where the light now is.

I may not be the person that I imagined I would become when I was younger, but I am discovering that is not necessarily a bad thing. Even though I don't like the change that grief has created in my life, I can't ignore these changes. I am adjusting to this new path I found myself on at twenty-seven. I want to see where this future without my mother will lead me, because it's the only future I have.

Being an adult isn't easy, and things never go according to plan, especially when you encounter loss. Now that I am an adult, I've finally realized the truth; adults don't have it all figured out. They don't know everything. The truth is adults are like children: they never stop growing.

CHAPTER 6

WHAT WOULD MARIE KONDO DO?

When my mother died, my aunt told me to pick the outfit we would bury her in. I went to my parent's closet and flipped through all her neglected dresses one by one. It had been a while since I'd seen them. After a few minutes, I picked a random purple, semiformal dress I had never seen her wear. When in doubt, semiformal seemed like a safe option for most events, including your own funeral.

When I came downstairs with my choice, my aunt told me to put it next to the packet of tea leaves, a mini teacup, and a newly bought blanket.

"What are all these for?" I asked my dad who was sitting nearby.

"They're for your mother. We're going to put them in the casket," my dad said.

Glancing at the teacup, I suddenly remembered when my mother woke up after her first tumor removal surgery. My aunt and dad immediately opened the thermos filled with tea, poured it into a similar teacup, and put it under my mother's nose so she could get a whiff of the strong oolong aroma. This was what comforted her when she woke up painfully in an unfamiliar place. *Would heaven smell like freshly brewed tea?*

"What's the blanket for?" I asked my dad.

"To keep her warm and safe," my dad answered.

I must have given him a look because he explained, "It's cold over there."

Unsure if he meant the place where she was going to be buried or the afterlife, I didn't bother correcting him on Biblical theology. Now was probably not the time to dispute cultural beliefs and start a discussion on whether she was "sleeping" until Jesus's second coming or if she went straight to heaven.

One week later, I would find myself in her closet again. This time, my dad wanted me to pack away her clothes.

Picking what items to bury with her was easy, but picking which items of hers to keep was going to be much harder.

My mother and I are sentimental hoarders. I keep every single card, even the ones I received in middle school from people I no longer talk to. Not surprisingly, I keep all my movie tickets. I would rather buy my ticket in-person for the ticket stub than purchase online. Like me, my mother kept random items. She had a small white bear sitting on her dresser. This was my favorite stuffed animal that I would bring everywhere with me when I was a child.

My dad, on the other hand, is often asking me if he can throw away my things. For instance, he once asked if he could discard all my artwork from middle school to high school, the last remaining reminders of how much I wanted to be an artist when I was younger. They were charcoal drawings, watercolor paintings, and oil paintings. They weren't anything you could showcase in a gallery, but I liked remembering how much I enjoyed drawing back then. I wanted to keep the past alive.

"Why?" I yelled a little too strongly at him.

"Well, we're not doing anything with them. They're just taking up space," he said.

It shouldn't have surprised me that my dad would not have been sentimental about my mother's belongings, especially her clothes. What was unexpected was how fast he wanted to put away her things.

In the first week after my mother's funeral, my dad responded to his grief by finding activities to occupy his time. He trimmed the hedges, replaced the curtains that covered the windows with blinds, and mowed the lawn. These were all the things my mother wanted him to do when she was alive, all the things he promised he would do but couldn't because he was taking care of her. He finally got to them after she died, and it only took him a few days. Once he was done, he decided to move on to her clothes.

It was too soon. I wanted to keep all her clothes untouched where they belonged, hanging in the closet and folded messily in the drawers. She may not have been physically around anymore, but I wanted to feel like she was still there, even if it wasn't true. I wanted to keep as much of her presence around as possible.

Afraid that he was going to throw away everything if I didn't get involved, I had no choice but to assist him with this task. He really needed all the help he could get because my mother had a lot of clothing.

As we piled all her clothes on my parents' bed and on the floor, I realized how long it had been since I had seen everything she used to wear. For the last year of her life, all my mother wore was pajamas or a night gown. Sometimes, she would wear a robe over her outfit. When she went to the hospital, she would just wear jeans, T-shirts, and a warm jacket. Nothing special.

I had forgotten how she used to stand in front of the mirror deciding what outfit to wear on Sunday mornings. After trying on a dress, she would move her hands down her sides to smooth any wrinkles. She would stare at the mirror, absorbed in whether she looked presentable for church. Sometimes she would wear a scarf, tying it in different ways or experimenting with different blazers or jackets to go with her outfit. For most of the week, she wore clothes that she knew would get dirty and grimy from working in a restaurant. She always came home smelling like fried rice and fried chicken. Sunday was the only day she could wear something nice.

Before she became ill, my mother liked to go to Macy's and outlet malls, searching for the best sales. My parents worked so much that they each only had capacity for one pastime. My dad followed football while my mom shopped. They often did their hobbies together. On Sundays, my dad would drive my mother to the mall while he waited in the parking lot listening to the game on the radio.

Once in the mall, my mother immediately headed to the back of the room where the discounted items were. She rarely bought things that weren't on sale. If we were to buy things that were the original price, they were usually for me. She was proud of the clothes she found on sale and excited when she had an opportunity to wear them. One time a family friend decided to take impromptu photos for my family during Christmas. My mother changed into four outfits while the rest of us just wore one. I can still see her beaming in an extravagant silver dress she wore only once to a wedding. Her clothes were her mark in the world, proof she had occasions to go to, something to celebrate.

I didn't realize how much I forgot about the person she was before her cancer. The last year of my mother's life was either spent at home or in hospitals. It was a year of finding clinical trials, emergency room visits, blood infusion treatments, and handling the logistics of my mother getting treated at multiple hospitals. Towards the end, her doctors tried to convince my dad and I to let my mother go on hospice as my mother's face became more sunken, her arms became twigs, and her legs swelled up. My dad and I were holding out for a miracle. We wanted to keep fighting this illness, but it was not our fight. The cancer had become a black hole within her, absorbing all the energy and life from her and leaving us with a person who was barely existing. My mother was tired from being unable to sleep because of the pain in her stomach and legs. She was tired of the clinical trials we wanted her to try. She was tired of being sick.

It wasn't until I saw all the clothes she used to wear that I remembered my mother used to be a healthy person who actually smiled and laughed. I forgot that she wasn't constantly in physical pain. I forgot that she could be happy.

We decided to do the easiest and quickest task first; throw away all the clothes she wore during the last moments of her life. These were the items that she donned when she could no longer bathe, eat, and drink anymore. We quickly stuffed the white night gown with red flower prints, the fuzzy pajama set, the fluffy robe, and all the beanies she wore in a clear plastic bag. No discussion needed. We didn't need any reasons to remember what she went through at the end. Too bad we couldn't discard the memories from the clothes as easily.

For the rest of her clothes, I needed to summon my inner Marie Kondo, the cleaning guru who inspired me to take care of my space more carefully and intentionally. Tidying is more than just cleaning your home; it's the continual act of learning how to let go of the things you don't need anymore and make better choices. From decluttering my personal items, I was able to understand myself better underneath all the material possessions that accumulated over time. Decluttering helped me to pause and reflect on the kind of life I was creating by examining my possessions carefully. What would I discover about my mother from the items that she left behind? Was there something that they could tell me that she couldn't? Was there anything left of my mother for me to discover?

To decide whether you should keep an item, Marie Kondo suggests you hold the item and see if it "sparks joy" (Kondo, 2011). For me, the spark is the instant jolt when you realize how much life there is still in the item. Most of the time, we don't think much about the items taking up space in our home. It is only when we are faced with the decision to remove them from our lives that we realize which items still serve a purpose, similar to how we don't realize how important a person is to us until they are at death's door.

This practice is a little different when you are examining another person's belongings, especially ones from someone who recently passed away. If she was still here, these items would merely just be her belongings, and I would barely give them any thought. When she died, all the clothes she left behind suddenly became precious overnight. They were tied to the past that I could no longer return to, mementos of a time that shouldn't have felt so far away. When I held her clothes in my hands, none of them sparked joy. They reminded me that I not only lost the ill person she became at the end but the once healthy and strong version of her as well. They triggered happier images of her that I had not seen in a long time and that I would never see again.

But remembering all the ways my mother was gone from the clothes she used to wear did not cut as deeply as the ones I never saw her wear. In my mother's drawers, I found shirts and dresses that still had the price tags on them. My mother had a habit of buying things she planned to use later but never did. On Black Fridays, she would go to the outlets and buy brand name purses for her relatives and friends in China. Every so often, she would keep one for herself. However, these new purses merely stayed in the back of the closet while she continued to use her old, tattered bag. This habit also extended to items she bought for me. My mother came back from China with a new blanket for me that she was saving to give me for my wedding. To this day, her gift is sitting in my parents' closet waiting for me to get married.

As I looked at the price tags, I thought of Margie, a widow who enlisted the help of Marie Kondo to tidy her home and late husband's belongings in the Netflix show *Tidying Up with Marie Kondo*. In episode four, Margie looks at her husband's side of the closet and says, "I thought about all the hopes and dreams he had when he was in his Hawaiian phase, and then when he was in his cowboy phase."

These new price tags were my mother's hopes and dreams. I may not have memories of my mother wearing the new dresses and shirts, but I saw pieces of an ordinary future she thought would come so easily. Days that would no longer come.

As I held onto the price tags, I recalled the sacrifices she made for me. I thought about the long hours she worked Monday through Saturday as a cashier for the food on our tables, the house we lived in, and the college I went to. I thought about how my parents always said they would take a vacation one day and how long my mother waited before she went to China to visit her relatives. After she passed away, my dad asked me, "What was it all for? Why did she work so hard? In the end, it was for nothing."

How long did she plan to wait before she pulled the price tags off? How long was she going to keep working until she could wear the new clothes she bought for herself? How long did she have to wait before she could do what she wanted?

These price tags were not evidence of a bad shopping habit but one of hope. They were the expectation that she was going to wear these new clothes one day, the anticipation of the days ahead. Now that she is gone, these price tags are mementos of her unfulfilled simple wishes and the confirmation of days that would never come.

What am I to do with all the hopes and dreams she left behind? Do I want to remember her hope for the future? Or do I want to throw away reminders of her dreams that will never come?

Sometimes it is hard to look beyond the grief, and all I can see in the things she left behind is our lost future that I naively believed was always guaranteed. However, as much as her things point to her absence in our lives, they remind me equally of how much she was once here. When I look at her things, I don't want to forget my past with her, even if it simultaneously makes me think of the days ahead without her.

As I made my way through her clothes, I tried to make the best decision that resulted in the least amount of regret. Did they spark joy in my memory of her, or did they not spark joy? Was a photo of her wearing the clothes enough? Could I bear to let go of this one memory of her, even if the memory is only of what she wore? Every time I come across something that belonged to my mother, I cannot escape the mental gymnastics of discerning whether to discard or keep her items.

Even in my grief, I am a sentimental hoarder. I am afraid of losing all the ways to remember her. Tossing an item feels like too much of a risk. What if by tossing an item, I lose a memory of my mother I can never regain? I can't bear to forgo any keepsake of the time we once shared. As time moves onward from my mother's death, I already feel pieces of my mother fading.

Since my room is located right next to the stairs, I became an expert at predicting who was making their way upstairs by the sound of their steps. My dad's footsteps are a heavy thump on each staircase since he tends to drag his feet. My grandmother's steps were slow, with a lot of pause in between each step. My aunt's are light and steady. I am no longer certain of what my mother's steps sounds like anymore, no matter how much I search my memory. What I missed the most is what came after the footsteps. My mother always stuck her head in my room briefly to greet me after she returned home from work.

I also can't remember what my mother's voice sounds like anymore. I know it wasn't particularly low or high. It wasn't husky or raspy. It was ordinary and mediocre as far as voices go. I miss hearing the affection in her voice when she called me "pig" in our Chinese dialect. It was the only voice that called me by that childhood nickname.

As these details about my mother start to get lost in time, I feel the distance between us growing. The more details about her I forget, the more of her I feel like I am losing. Death pulled my mother and me apart. I didn't realize it could also pull away the things I knew about her as well. What will I have left of my mother five years from now? Ten years? Twenty years?

Keeping all her items seemed like a good solution to prevent her from disappearing altogether. However, I get the feeling that Marie Kondo would still advise against keeping everything, no matter how kind and gentle she is. I cannot hold onto everything for a person who is no longer here and who is not coming back. Hoarding all her items would prevent me from confronting reality. I will never move on from my mother, but I must continue onward without her.

One recurring theme that ran through the episode with Margie was that she didn't have anyone to consult with anymore about the decisions she had to make. She was the sole decision maker now in the house. Marie Kondo gently encouraged Margie to believe that she was capable of making decisions on her own. Margie was the expert on all the things in her home. No one could tell her what to do with her items, even her husband's things.

After watching Marie Kondo's show, I can see why people's houses get messy and start to accumulate items over time. It is hard making decisions about the future. How do we know what items to keep? What if we throw away something we will need later? How do we have the confidence to know we are making the right decisions for our future?

These questions continue to persist in my grief. What do I need to remember my mother by? What can I let go? How do I keep her here with me while creating the space for us to acknowledge her absence?

After deciding what items to throw away, I wasn't sure if I had the confidence to decide what items to keep as mementos, to donate or give away, or to keep for my own personal use.

During the whole process, my father barely said anything. He quietly helped me put away the clothes once we decided which category they belonged to. If he had any response to the clothes that she used to wear, I didn't know. The only sound he made was a sigh of agreement when my aunt exclaimed "how tragic" in response to all the new clothes my mother bought. Unlike Margie who had tears when she went through her husband's clothes, my father, aunt, and I shed no tears. My dad also stayed quiet when I chose key pieces to remember her by. He didn't question whether I chose too many or too little clothes to keep. Looking back, his silence was his trust that I would make the right decisions with what to do with her remaining items.

In the decluttering process, I was able to discover something about myself and my mother underneath all her clothes. Like Margie, I learned that I can trust myself when it comes to making these small ordinary decisions. I will trust in myself like how my father trusted in me with my mother's possessions. I need to be confident as the keeper of my mother's life. Someday, the details about my mother will fade, but there are some things time can never touch: the love between my mother and me. Even though I have lost her physically, I have not lost the love that she left behind. Her love is not in her clothes or her belongings; it is in me. And that can never be discarded.

More importantly, I know I can trust this love that was given to me for the rest of my life. Someday the details of my mother will fade; that is inevitable. Instead of hoarding every reminder of her, I hope that I will be brave enough to let go when the time comes because I don't have to be afraid of losing the temporary things when I already have the eternal and everlasting treasures. Material possessions won't last forever. Even our memories can leave us with time. The people and the things on Earth will one day be gone, but the heavenly things like love and truth will last forever. These are the things my mother trusted in, and this is what I choose to trust in as well.

CHAPTER 7

THE COST OF DYING

My mother was not the first person I saw die. When I was ten, my grandmother on my father's side died the same way. In the middle of the living room, she took her last breath surrounded by all her loved ones. Like my grandmother, my mom would die from cancer in her living room with the same people by her side.

After the funeral, my mother started pinning a tiny white ribbon to me every day before I went to school.

"Why are you wearing that ribbon?" my friends would ask me.

I shrugged, unsure myself. Eventually, I forgot about it, and after a period of time, my mom stopped pinning it on me. It wasn't until my mother's funeral that I realized it must have been a Chinese custom to symbolize mourning.

Since I was born and raised in America, many Chinese customs went unnoticed by me. Most of the time I attributed them to my parents' peculiarities rather than my culture. For instance, it is a superstition among Chinese people to not say bad things out loud for fear of them happening. This is why we never talk about death or illness, even when we face it ourselves. And why I couldn't talk about the potential of not getting married, because my mother was afraid that if I mentioned any possibility of being single, it would come true. I eventually realized that the fear of saying bad things out loud was not a unique practice in my household, but a common practice among Chinese people.

I didn't think much of these cultural customs because they didn't really impact my life. They were merely sayings and beliefs that my parents had. It wasn't until my mother's funeral that all my parents' cultural customs began to matter, overwhelming every decision I needed to make. Preparing and planning for my mother's funeral would teach me a lot about my culture, more so than any other time in my life.

Once my mother went on hospice, many people encouraged us to get a head start on making her funeral arrangements. I didn't see how this would make my grieving any easier, but I suppose anytime there's less logistics to handle, the less stress there is. It's probably better to be grieving than to be grieving and stressing.

In my preparation, the very first thing I learned was that Chinese people have very strong preferences for where the grave site is. I thought that it didn't matter where you were buried, as long as you had a place to lie. Apparently, the direction the grave faces matters. I was told that the tombstone should face west, but I also heard my mother's friend say, "But, it doesn't really matter if it faces west because she was born in the year of the dog."

Days later, when I was at the memorial park to sign the paper for my mother's burial site, I asked someone there why Chinese people wanted their graves to face west. He shrugged and said, "Maybe, it is because China lies across the Pacific Ocean."

People never seemed to want to forget where they came from.

My question didn't seem to strike the worker as odd. They were used to all the intricate ways my ancestors like to bury the dead. Whether Chinese or not, the staff there knew more about the traditions from my culture than I did. It was obvious that some of the sites were created intentionally with feng shui in mind. Some areas even had a Chinese name and statues of dragons at the entrance. People are usually willing to pay more to keep their traditions alive. It shouldn't have surprised me to learn that not only is the cost of living expensive in the Bay Area but the cost of dying as well.

The average cost of a burial plot in California is $5,545. ("Cemetery Burial Plot Cost in California," 2021) Land is expensive whether you're living on it or buried in it. Besides the plot, you must also purchase the outer burial vault to contain the casket. Gone are the days where you could just bury a person in a coffin. You now need a vault to keep the ground from settling to maintain the beauty of the memorial park. But don't worry, they have different price ranges for the vaults, depending on how much you want to invest in protecting your loved one's remains. The tombstone, endowment care fund, and processing fees are also included when purchasing the land.

And of course, you can't bury a person without a funeral service and casket. (Nope, the casket is not included with buying the land.) Fortunately, the memorial site offers you a package that includes visitation, death certificates, embalming, a diverse selection of caskets, funeral hearse and flower vehicle use, dressing and casketing of the deceased, transferring the remains to the funeral home, and more. You just can't seem to escape capitalism, even in death.

Growing up with frugal parents, I thought we would want to find somewhere affordable for my mother, especially since we had to purchase two burial plots and two funeral packages: one for my mother and one that would eventually belong to my father. If we didn't save my dad's spot, someone else would take it. And wouldn't that be awkward to be buried next to someone who wasn't your spouse?

After calling different memorial sites, I found a somewhat affordable plot across the Bay. If it were up to me, I would have purchased it right away without needing to visit. After all, don't all plots of land look the same? It was probably no different than the grass on my front lawn. However, my dad and uncle who went to see the plot managed to find problems with the one I chose. Fortunately, there was someone at the memorial park to show them more options. Unfortunately, it was not the same price.

"What? Why did you choose the more expensive one?" I asked my dad.

"Because, the one you told us about is in a bad place. It's all the way down at the bottom of a slope where the cemetery wall is. When it rains, all the water will go there," my uncle told me.

Unsure why that was an issue, I responded with a bewildered look.

"Do you really want your mom to be drenched in water?" my dad asked me.

I supposed not.

Wanting this process to be finished, I decided to not say anything and just let him be happy with his choice while I made the plans to purchase it.

"You don't have to pay for it all at once. You can pay it in installments," the family service advisor from the memorial park told me when she sensed my hesitancy.

"Oh, really?" I said as I began making mental calculations of how much to subtract from my savings.

"Yes, but once the person dies, you have to pay for all of it," she added.

"Well, we don't know when my mom will die. Who knows? Maybe we will still have a few months," I said as hopefully as I could.

Less than a week later, I would contact her to pay the full cost.

As we discussed how I wanted to pay for my mother's funeral arrangements, I remembered the promises I made to my mother when I was younger. Well, more like, I remembered the promises she told me I made to her. My mom used to tell me often that I promised her when I was a child that I would buy her a red car and a mansion one day. I'm not sure why she liked retelling that story. Did she really expect me to buy her those things? When I made her those promises, what kind of future did she envision for me to purchase those gifts?

Being the only child of immigrant parents meant they put all their hopes and dreams in me to succeed. My parents thought I could do anything, simply because "you were born here."

For instance, they often thrust government and financial forms in my face and said, "Here, fill out this form for us quickly. You should be able to do it fast since you were born here."

When I became stumped by the instructions on the paperwork, they would be surprised. In response, they asked, "What? Why are you frustrated? This should be easy for you, since you were born here."

To my parents, my birth in this country and grasp of the English language meant I had a higher chance of being successful, especially compared to when they first came to this country.

When my grandpa was a child, his parents put him and his stepsister on a train that traveled from China to Vietnam. They hoped that they would have a better life living with his aunt and uncle than in China where there was a famine. He would never see his parents again. Decades later, my grandpa, his wife, and seven children would escape their home country during the Vietnam War and become refugees in the place I was born and raised. Even though my dad's family was more settled by the time my mother moved from China when she married my dad, life didn't get easier. They still needed to figure out how to raise a family from the wages of working in food service, a grueling and risky industry.

When I was born, my parents continued working hard to give me a stable home to raise me in. Because of their resilience, I never had to struggle like they did. They made sure of that. All they wanted me to do was study, receive good grades, and get accepted to a good college. Oh, and fill out those government forms quickly for them.

Fortunately, my studies paid off and I went to college. However, I returned home to one of the most expensive cities in the country to work for a nonprofit. Sometimes, my mother would randomly look at me and say, "You know when you were younger, I always thought you would go to Stanford and become a doctor."

Every time I responded the same way: an eye roll. I never took her words personally because I knew that my parents were never truly tiger parents, like some of my friends had. Tiger parents knew their child's grades, even better than the child themselves, and the teacher. They made sure to monitor their children's schedule so that their time was spent studying and on extracurricular activities, rather than having fun or, worse, being unproductive. My parents were too busy working to track my studies. It was clear to me that they wanted me to work hard, so that I could find a job that wouldn't require me to labor as intensely as they did.

I supposed I should have felt guilty for not having a higher paying job after all the sacrifices they made to provide for me. I thought eventually I would find a job that they could be proud of—I would just take my time getting there or marry rich—whichever came first. I thought I would have time to make up for their sacrifices.

I know my mother didn't really care whether I could buy her the red car and mansion or not. Those things were just her dreaming for me to have a successful future. They were my dreams too. Not so much the material items, but I had hoped that I could show my parents that I was capable of providing for them when they grew older. Even though I wasn't at the point where I could buy her a red car or mansion (though the latter was extremely unlikely), I should have taken more opportunities to show my appreciation. I may not have made as much as those in Silicon Valley, but I still could have bought her something, anything.

There were so many things that I wanted to buy her: purses, dinners, jewelry, vacations, clothes. I never got to splurge on something for my mother. Instead of buying all the things I could have, should have, and would have, I bought her a grave site. This would be my most expensive purchase for her. Not the red car. Not the mansion. Not even a purse. My last and final gift would be the plot of land where we buried her.

Unsurprisingly, the second thing I learned about funeral customs was that money was somehow involved. Not only do Chinese people love to give red envelopes with money in them on Chinese New Year, birthdays, weddings, and other celebrations, but at funerals as well. For the funeral, we gave everyone a red envelope with a new, crisp dollar bill and candy so that they could leave the burial site with something sweet. The funeral worker even asked if I wanted to prepare red envelopes with money to put on the windshield of the cars of the guests. Because China was so big, there are so many different versions of customs that come from all over. I decided to pass on the windshield custom since we were already doing something similar.

Thankfully, we wouldn't be the only ones giving money. It was expected that people would give us money as well. One of the first things someone recommended I do is get a box for the money and a book to record how much people gave. Initially, I thought this was a strange recommendation, but I realized how helpful it was after the funeral when we wanted to send thank you letters. When I opened the envelopes, I noticed an odd trend in the amount that people gave. Many gave us money in amounts that ended with the number 1, like $101, $501, etc. The additional dollar was to ensure that their amount was an odd number to indicate that you didn't want the spouse that was still alive to join the dead one. In comparison, you should only give even number amounts for weddings to show that you wanted the couple to be together. Whether people gave us an odd or even number amount, I was grateful that we broke even for the funeral service cost.

The third thing I learned is the timeless lesson that communication is key. At the funeral, my mother received many large flower arrangements from relatives in Hong Kong and

China. Since they couldn't be here, I made the purchase for them. As I was ordering the flowers, my uncle gave me the Chinese characters of the names of distant relatives from my dad's side to include on the ribbons, so we knew who sent them. My aunt did the same for my mother's side. It was strange buying flowers for relatives I couldn't put a face to.

On the day of the funeral, my grandparents on my dad's side were surprised to discover that none of the flower arrangements had my dad's siblings' names on them. Half an hour before the funeral, they asked me if I could still make the order. The person at the flower shop told me they could send more flowers, but they couldn't prepare the ribbons in time. I passed this along to my grandmother, who told me we couldn't have the flowers without the ribbons. I'm not sure why the ribbons were so important. It must have been a typical practice that people in China did for their relatives to show their support during this difficult time. Later, the ribbons with peoples' names would be cut off right before they placed the flowers on top of her grave. I never did ask why the ribbons needed to be cut, but I assumed keeping the ribbons with your name still intact on the flower arrangements for the dead is bad luck.

One day before the funeral, I realized that I needed about eight pallbearers and asked the relatives who were visiting if they could be one. My cousins said they could do it, as well as some of my uncles. However, when I asked my great uncle to be a pallbearer, he was caught off-guard and said that he couldn't do it. I found out later that it wasn't customary for someone older than my mother to be a pallbearer—that was reserved for those who were younger. Another thing that wasn't customary was for a child to die before her parents. This was the very reason why all my mother's relatives in

China insisted that my grandmother on my mother's side shouldn't be there to see the burial of her child.

Another grave mistake I found out weeks after the funeral was that we buried my mother on the wrong side. The wife is supposed to be buried on the left side and the husband on the right side. I'm sure if I wanted to move her to the correct side, the memorial site would probably have obliged with a fee (of course).

Curious, I asked my dad, "Why did we decide to bury her on the right side?"

My dad shrugged, "Well, I didn't want her to be close to the road. I figured I could protect her if I was on the left side."

My dad's rationale made so much more sense to me than all the customs and traditions that went into planning her funeral. Despite all the efforts my father and I put into keeping up with traditions, they didn't matter to us. We had never planned a funeral before and were merely going with the advice of others. Plus, it was easier getting absorbed into the details of the event than thinking about her death.

If my mother could attend her own funeral, is this what she would have wanted? How much did she care about honoring the beliefs of her ancestors and culture? Did these things matter to her?

As I contemplated how much effort I should put into keeping these traditions alive, a scene from *Kim's Convenience*, a Canadian show about a Korean immigrant family that owns a convenience store, kept playing in my mind. In the scene, a customer asked the parents to sign a petition to get a better playground for the neighborhood. Initially, they enthusiastically agreed to sign the petition until they were handed a red pen. The women with the petition noticed their hesitancy and asked if there was a problem.

The father explained, "In Korea, when you die, they write your name in red."

"Name in red means you is dead," the mother added.

The woman responded by saying, "I'm so sorry, I didn't know Koreans were so superstitious."

"Many Koreans is superstitious," the mother said defensively, "but we is Christian, and Christian is not superstitious."

To back up her claim, the father says he will sign the petition. As he starts to write his signature, he presses on the pen so hard that the top breaks. Feigning apologetic expressions, they quickly replace the red pen with a black one to sign the petition. Breaking traditions can be just as hard as breaking habits.

Even though red is a lucky color for Chinese people, we also don't like signing in red for a similar reason relating to death. I learned this at a young age when I would hand my mother a red pen to sign my permissions slips. She would immediately find a different color pen.

Besides the similar superstition, my mother would also respond the same way as the Korean mother in the show when I questioned why she did things a certain way. After she explained the custom to me, she would pause and then immediately add a disclaimer, "But we are Christian now, so we don't believe in these things."

It is not that my mother was throwing away the beliefs she was raised in for the new faith she found in America. This is not her way of giving up her culture and assimilating into a new one. My mother was still very Chinese to the core. She would give me disapproving looks whenever I drank anything cold. She washed the plates and chopsticks with the hot water at dim sum restaurants, not trusting how well they cleaned the utensils. She would rather believe the information she learned from Wechat (China's biggest social media platform) than anything I had to say. There was so much about the American culture and language that she didn't understand or try to understand.

All the things she was told about how to avoid death and bad luck didn't make sense anymore when you knew who was ultimately in control of your life. There was nothing to be afraid of when you know that Jesus awaits us in heaven. Becoming Christian didn't mean that she had to let go of the culture she was raised in but looking at the culture with a new lens.

However, just because you learned something new doesn't mean you can break old habits or traditions so easily. Like the parents in *Kim's Convenience,* my mother was still uncomfortable signing in red even though she knew it was a superstition. It is in this tension that I tried to navigate all the decisions that went into honoring my mother's heritage and our Christian faith.

As I thought about which traditions were necessary to uphold, I started to wonder who I was organizing this funeral for anyway. My mother is no longer here to guide me on the traditions of our culture. She was gone. And we were left with her body to bury.

Why did it matter that we keep these traditions passed down from my ancestors alive?

I realized that these beliefs were not just a way to honor the dead, but they were how their loved ones mourned their loss. Putting a blanket in the casket wasn't just so they could ensure their loved one was warm in the afterlife; it was a tiny mental comfort to believe they could still provide for their loved one somehow. Is this how I wanted to mourn, when I didn't believe in these things?

Does it really matter how my mother's funeral went? Was there anything I would regret doing or not?

My mother was gone.

Why did these things matter? Why did I have to care about what other people wanted? Who was I doing this for in the end?

"You have to be more humble," I can hear my mother saying. This was my mother's favorite phrase to say to me in every situation. I used to get incredibly frustrated with her for saying this before she let me explain my side of the story. However, she was right, as usual. If I really examined my heart, I know that the source of most of my problems was my pride.

This funeral wasn't entirely about me and my loss. Funerals are for the grievers. They aren't for the dead, but for those who are still alive to mourn at the same time and place as others. It is the start of the separation from your loved one, the painful realization and acknowledgment that your loved one is no longer here. I wasn't the only one grieving. This funeral was for everyone that loved her, and whether Christian or not, I didn't want to disregard their input. These cultural customs may not have mattered to me, but they mattered to some of the people she loved. They mattered to my relatives in China who believed strongly that my grandmother should not attend her funeral. They mattered to my relatives who weren't Christian and still believed in having certain traditions set in place.

Trying not to overthink every little detail, I honored the traditions where I could without compromising my Christian convictions. Her funeral wasn't a war zone between her heritage and her faith. It was the place where the people she loved came together to honor her with their best intentions. This was the battleground for where hearts break and love hurts. We needed all the support we could have from each other.

As the coordinator for her funeral, I have to say it turned out as well as funerals could go. All the cultural conditions that were included did not ultimately impact the service itself when the pastor spoke, Bible verses were read, and her favorite Christian songs were sung.

Oddly, it was good for me to see people sad and mourning, to know that they would miss her, that she was important to people. It was good to miss my mother with others, to not be alone as we buried her. Funerals really aren't for the dead, but the ones they loved.

Most importantly, I used my eulogy to do what I believe my mother would have wanted, to share the Gospel with the people she loved who didn't know Christ. Since her relatives couldn't be there, my aunt's friend recorded the ceremony for our family members in China who were not Christian. Taking advantage of the fact that there would be someone translating my words, I did the best I could to share Christ with all the people she loved who attended. This was the one thing I was confident and sure about, that my mother wanted her loved ones to hear the Gospel. I never did tell my mother how much I admired her passion, bravery, and persistence when it came to sharing the Gospel. Instead, I tried to emulate her at her funeral, channeling her fiery power for Christ, honoring her best trait. This was who my mother was, and I was proud to be her daughter.

My mother's funeral would not be the last time I went to the memorial park. It was the first of many visits. We visited her two weeks later for Mother's Day, her birthday in September, and then every holiday after that until her death anniversary. To this day, we have repeated this pattern more than twice already. I plan to continue visiting my mother often. After all, I have to get my money's worth of the land.

Every time we visit the park, I appreciate my dad's decision to choose the expensive burial site more and more. Originally, purchasing this site was something that needed to be done. There wasn't much significance to this place because it wasn't where my mother resided, no matter how many times I told my friends and coworkers that I was "visiting" my mother. This was where she was buried. She was not anywhere anymore, so how could she be there? My mother was in heaven, and I was on Earth. Her burial site was not the magical gateway that connected us or where I felt her presence more.

However, the more I went there, the fonder I grew of the place. On a cloudless day, if you look straight ahead towards the west where her tombstone faces, you see the big blue ocean sitting between two green hills. At first, I thought the ocean was the sky. They were the same color blue, and I couldn't tell where they met. If you're lucky, you will get to see a family of deer meandering through the tombstones, nibbling at the grass and flowers left for loved ones. If she was buried in the original place, we would miss the scene of the sky and the deer because we would be surrounded by a wall.

Just like the funeral, the burial site isn't for the dead but for the grievers. It is here that my family builds our own traditions. The night before each visit, my dad buys two bouquets of flowers from Costco. We get up unnecessarily early. My dad always thinks I will sleep in, but I am ready to go in the morning. We get a latte for me as we make the drive to the park. Once there, my dad puts the flowers in the vase and cleans her grave. He finds her favorite worship songs on YouTube and plays them on his phone. Last, we pour her favorite tea on the grave.

No matter how many times my dad tells me to say goodbye to her before we leave, I don't feel it is necessary. She can't see or hear me at the place where we buried her. But it is here at this grave site where we remember her in these ordinary moments, and I don't ever want to stop.

CHAPTER 8

THE THIRD ACT

"You may want to get a recording of her voice or a message from her," my aunt told me during the last six months of my mother's life.

When she first made the suggestion, I wasn't sure how to respond and whether I should follow through. It wasn't a terrible idea and seemed like something my future self might want. But I couldn't do it. It felt like admitting defeat. I was too stubborn to acknowledge that we were at the end and didn't want to confront what it would mean to live without her. I wasn't brave enough to ask my mother for a piece of her that would one day soon be gone.

From this fear of the future, it was not surprising how the third act of my mother's and my story turned out. My TV habits should have clued me in on how I would have handled the conclusion of her arc in my life. I know my way of watching Asian dramas or American TV shows is a bit baffling and abnormal; I leave a majority of them unfinished. Even though I rave about the shows that I am currently watching, it is rare for me to make it to the finale or the last season of the series. My typical pattern starts with getting hooked on a show first from the trailer. This is what I call the "love at first sight" stage. I rewatch the trailer many times, impatiently waiting to explore the world and meet the characters. If they win me over by the third episode, I become completely invested as I fall deeply for the characters, plot, and world. However, as I make my way toward the end, I start to feel reluctant to watch the next few episodes. I start making excuses, and eventually, I stop watching the show altogether. This weird phenomenon is due to my reluctance to part with the characters and world I've grown to love over the past few weeks. If I don't finish the series, I don't have to say goodbye. Another reason is that I've been let down many times by poor endings. I can't bear to watch the characters I love get a rushed or underwhelming ending.

If only I had the courage to face endings, then maybe I could have confronted my mother's third act more boldly and intentionally. My dad and I were so absorbed in keeping my mother with us that we did not realize the ending of her life was being written.

Before we get to the third act, let me tell you about the first act. The last chapter of my mother's life started with her ovarian cancer's return. In the beginning, we were scared but determined to fight this villain of our story together. We would soon discover that there were no victories this time, only losses. My mother didn't respond well to the chemotherapy. The radiation didn't help either. It just made her weaker. It was a battle trying to find a clinical trial that would accept her. Once we finally found one that would take her, she had a bad reaction that ended with us in the emergency room and the hospital for a couple of days. We should have stopped there and tried to make the best out of every moment while she was still with us. Instead, we grew more desperate for another treatment, for more time.

In between, there were many tests to see if the medications were working. When I was in high school, I dreaded going to the back of the room where the test results were posted. As everyone crowded at the posted sheet, I didn't mind waiting from far away. I was afraid to look at my test results and see how they would impact my grade and eventually my future. I didn't realize that there were more fatal test results, ones that determine how much longer you have left in your future. All the hopes I had in getting good grades were nothing compared to the hope that I had for the results of my mother's blood work to be in the normal range.

By the time we made it to the second act, my mother's body became frailer and more damaged from each treatment she underwent. With each disappointing test result, she became more defeated while my father and I became more frantic that there were fewer and fewer options for her. When we met with the final doctor we reached out to, he took one look at her and told us she was not strong enough for any more trials or treatment. Naturally, my dad and I walked out of that appointment feeling discouraged and upset. *How could he tell us so easily that that was it? How could he tell us to stop fighting for my mother's life? How could he tell us to let go?*

"You know what I felt when he told me that?" my mother asked us that evening.

"What?" I asked, afraid of what she was going to say next.

"So relieved that I don't have to go to hospitals anymore. Or try any new treatment," she told us.

My dad and I didn't know how to respond, but we knew we weren't ready to give up and watch her die. At that time, I thought she was only tired from fighting the cancer, an enemy that wouldn't relent. I didn't realize it may have been more tiring to be around people who wouldn't listen to you.

By now we are entering the third act where the conclusion starts to take place. This is when we would start having the tough but touching conversations. She would tell me how much she loved me or how proud she was of me. Then, she would pass along instructions, wisdom, or advice for me. For instance, she might say things like, "don't fight with your dad when I am not around," and make me promise that we would always take care of each other. Cue the cheesy soundtrack music and tears.

Or maybe she would tell me about her childhood in China, something I never thought to ask her more about. I would find out who she was before she came to America, who she was before she was my mother. I would discover all her hopes and dreams from her youth. Perhaps, I might discover a dark harbored family secret or two. This would have been the moment to record her voice.

She did no such things. There was no advice, no confessions or declaration of her love or pride for me. She didn't tell us how happy we made her or how much she didn't want to leave us. She just stayed quiet and waited. Unlike my dad and I, she knew she was dying.

My dad and I were so preoccupied with avoiding the truth and trying to find options for her that we didn't realize how withdrawn she had become until it was too late. She only had energy to tell us how much pain she was in or how uncomfortable she was. Anything beyond that would be too much for her. Besides, why bother talking to people who weren't listening to you?

Why did it take so long for me to realize how much there was about my mother that I didn't know? Why did I realize how much more I wanted to know my mother only after she was gone?

Why did things always have to be too late?

Before, I never thought too much about what kind of person my mother was. She was my mother, and nothing else. As I became an adult, I started to realize that she was not only my mother but a person too. She was filled with mistakes, mysteries, regrets, hopes, dreams, and everything else that makes a person human. There was so much about her that I didn't know, an entire universe left unexplored. And vice versa. There were many things about myself she did not know, many things I could have told her but didn't. All these details and tidbits about ourselves were supposed to come out more organically as we got older and as I matured. I didn't know that there would be an end to our relationship, an end to know who she was and is.

Would it have made a difference if my family confronted her death more directly? If we talked to each other more, if we told each other how much we loved each other and were going to miss each other, would there be less regret now? Would grief be less painful? Would anything change?

Even though it is tempting to go down the rabbit hole of "what-ifs," I do not like wasting time and mental energy thinking about the things that I cannot change. My mother is gone whether we talked about her death or not, whether we told each other we loved each other at the end or not. My mother is gone, no matter what I did or didn't do.

Even though this third act is a little depressing, I have a hard time imagining it could be any different. Learning how to be so open about our feelings with one another is not something we were accustomed to. This would be a practice that would take years to learn and develop—years we didn't have.

But this is typical of my family; we are poor verbal communicators. We never say what we mean, and we never mean what we say.

For the longest time, my parents would often get upset whenever I cut my fingernails at night. Once, my dad said angrily to me, "I can't believe you waited until the end of the day to cut your nails. What were you doing before that you couldn't cut your nails until now?"

I didn't understand why my dad was so upset. The only conclusion I could come up with is that he was insulting my time-management skills since I chose to cut my nails at the end of the day. It was so unnecessary for him to get mad at me over such an ordinary task.

Before I could defend myself, my aunt suddenly said, "A lot of people say that it is bad to cut your nails at night. It can bring bad things."

After years of misunderstanding, I finally realized that they were upset because of a Chinese superstition, not because of me. I never thought there was a reasonable (or unreasonable) explanation for why they became so upset when I cut my nails. I never asked, and they never explained. There were so many unsaid things between us that we didn't know needed to be said out loud.

Despite all the things we didn't say to each other, there was one thing I never had to question: my mother's love for me.

She did not need to tell me she loved me in words. Other people would do it for her. Relatives often told me, "Your mom worries about you so much. She is always thinking of you."

This was very clear to me, especially in college when my mother would call me every single night for the entire four years. She never skipped a night. Here is the exact transcript of our conversation.

Me: Hello?

Mom: Where are you?

Me: I'm in my apartment.

Mom: Okay, good night.

If I wasn't in my apartment, she would tell me to go home. According to her, it was dangerous to be out at night no matter where you lived. Sometimes, she might ask me if I ate dinner already or if I needed money. My mother rarely asked me what I did that day or how I was doing. She didn't need to know those details. She just wanted to know I was alive and well.

I was not raised on physical or verbal displays of affections. I was raised by my parents asking me if I ate every time I came home and telling me to put on a jacket when I went outside so that I wouldn't catch a cold. My parents never asked me how school went or if there was anything I was struggling with. Instead, they peeled and sliced fruit for me every night when I was studying or doing my homework. My parents stopped hugging or holding me once I became too big to pick up. Instead, my mother would bring a cup of warm water to my room every night before I slept, and my dad would get up early to go to Costco to fill my tank of gas without me asking.

What would it have been like if we loved with our words?

Would I have been able to tell my mother all the things I wish we could have done together and all the things I wish I did for her? Would I have told her how much I was going to miss her, how sorry I was for being so stubborn and selfish, how thankful I was for all the sacrifices she made for me? Would I have been able to tell her how much I knew she cared for me and how much I cared for her?

Would it have mattered in the end to confirm all the things we already knew?

No, it wouldn't have mattered because I did not need my mother to tell me she loved me to know that it was true. My mother did not sacrifice so much for me to not know how much she loved me. There may be many unsaid things between us, but that will never change what we've always known and trusted about each other: our love.

At the same time, I wonder if we were able to say the things in our hearts, where would that lead us? What other things could we tell each other? If we developed the habit of talking more openly and often, then maybe I would have a fuller picture of who my mother was. Before, I only thought to ask her for permission, rarely for her opinion. Now I wish I could know her thoughts on all the decisions I am making without her. All the things that went on in her mind and heart are forever lost; along with that is all our missed opportunities at having a deeper understanding of each other.

It's like her life ended on a cliffhanger at the end of a season, but the writers never brought her back for the next season. All the things that were supposed to occur with her story line are forever lost. I will never know what was supposed to happen to her and to us. There was no neat ending, no tightly written conclusion—only loose ends that I keep picking at.

I try not to think about how I wanted our third act to go. It would hurt too much. But I know that I should have listened to what she wanted or at least apologized for how much I wanted her to keep fighting until the end. I wish my dad and I knew that it was never our battle to begin with. It was hers all along.

I wanted to be next to my mother, holding her hand until the very last moment. But I had to eat lunch.

On the day my mother died, her good friend from church came to pray with us. We surrounded her bed and each one of us prayed for her. After we finished, everyone decided to step away from her bed for a little bit. This was one of the rare times she was left alone that day. My dad went to the couch to try and get a quick nap. I went to the dining table ten feet from where my mom slept to eat the lunch my cousin brought us.

The doorbell suddenly rang as I was eating and talking to my cousin.

My uncle's family had arrived. After they said their greetings, my aunt went over to my mother. She immediately started crying and told us she passed away.

My dad likes to say, "She quickly took her chance when no one was around."

My mother was always thinking of us, even in the last moments of her life. She didn't want us to be around her to see her pass. My mother fought for as long as she could—not for herself but for us. She was sacrificial to the very end.

You were amazing. You fought so hard for us.

I finally found the words that I wanted to tell her all along, but she is no longer here.

This was how my family dealt with death. We were people who did not understand how to handle dying people and death … *handling* dying people and death. This is how I will have to leave it in my memory: imperfect people loving imperfect people.

However, all is not lost. There is a tiny bit of closure in our third act. My mother did leave me with a few words to cherish. A few months before she died, I went downstairs to check on my mother after praying for her in my room. Everyone was asleep but us. Even though her eyes were closed, I could tell she was still awake by how scrunched up her face was. I took her hand and then slowly said, "No one will ever love me as much as you do."

She opened her eyes, looked at me, and said, "God does."

Then she closed her eyes, and that was the end of our conversation.

This was the closest we got to talking about the future without her, the most direct way I told her I would miss her and that I loved her. And she answered in the most comforting way. She did not need to confirm or remind me about how much she loved me. We already knew how much we loved each other. Instead, she reminded me that I was not going to be alone after she was gone. God was still going to continue loving me afterward, and this love was so much greater than hers.

This was all her love, wisdom, and legacy wrapped up in these two words. And despite how much I wish I could have more, they will be enough to carry me through all the days of my life. Even though I love my mom so selfishly and stubbornly, God still gave me grace in those two words. And He continues to give me grace by not leaving me as I am. I will grow from the depths of the grief He left me with.

That is what we can do with the grief given to us: learn from it.

Fortunately, my mother was not the only person in my life who loved me. I am still my dad's favorite child (because I am his only one). My aunt and grandmother on my mother's side are still living with us. Despite my poor Chinese and my dad's and grandmother's poor hearing, I can still converse with them and discover what kind of people they are. We may not be telling each other how much we love each other or displaying physical affection anytime soon. We are still here, but we won't be here forever. Eventually, everyone I love will die, and I want to do my best in getting to know the people God has placed in my life while I still can.

It's hard breaking the habit of running from the third act, but I don't want to miss the ending anymore. I want to know what happens.

CHAPTER 9

THE OTHER SIDE OF GRIEF

"Do you feel better now?" is something you might ask someone after they told you they were recovering from a cold. It is also an appropriate question to ask someone who is finally taking their first bite of food after showing symptoms of hangry-ness. Or something you ask when a coffee addict finally takes their first sip of coffee that day.

It's not something you ask when you see someone for the first time after their brother passed away. Unfortunately, knowing that did not stop me from asking.

What I actually wanted to say was, "How are you doing with your grief? How do you feel? Is there anything I can do to help?"

Three simple questions that anyone could ask.

Instead, I asked a question that made it seem as if she was recovering from a cold, as if a few weeks was all she needed to "feel better now." You never feel better. Grief doesn't let you.

Clearly, experiencing grief does not make me more knowledgeable about loss or comfortable around others like myself. This is not a club you happily welcome people to or try to gain more membership in. When I was asking grief experts if I could interview them for my book, one of them responded to my email with "So, while I'm happy you found us, I wish you never needed to."

What an appropriate thing to say. Perfect words hand-picked together that made me feel welcomed, understood, and sad all at once. Words that demonstrated her experience in encountering other grievers.

Before my mother passed away, I didn't know what to say when I encountered a griever. However, I thought I knew exactly what not to say. I would not bring up their loss. Instead, I would ask them surface-level and indirect questions and let them decide how they wanted to respond. It only made sense for the grievers to initiate grief into the conversation. I would follow their lead and follow them wherever the discussion would go. A part of me was also hoping that they wouldn't bring it up because I didn't feel equipped to handle the conversation if it took a turn for the worse.

This was what I wanted in the beginning, too, when it was my turn to face loss—for people to not probe and to give me all the space that I wanted to adjust to this huge shift in my life. And there really was nothing to say. My mother was here and now is gone. She is never coming back. What else can I say?

But the words eventually came, even if I wasn't ready to share them or people weren't ready to hear. As I learned how to navigate this new world without my mother, all the words that I thought I didn't have began to fill and collect inside of me, waiting to spill over. The words that amassed were the result of all the painful discoveries of the old and new places my mother no longer occupied, all the realizations she was never returning, and all the clashes of what once was and what can no longer be. So many words sprouted in all the nooks and hidden passageways inside of me, places where I didn't know they could grow.

Slowly, these words poured out, finding their way outside of me and into the world. First, they showed up as comments I made whenever someone triggered a thought about her. If they knew my mother passed away, they usually pause and wait, unsure of what to say next. Maybe they were on the verge of saying something, but they usually said nothing at all. They waited patiently for the conversation to return to its previous course. Sometimes, I wonder if they heard me mention my mother at all.

So, this is what it's like to be on the other side.

I thought my silence was helpful, that it was the right etiquette to not mention their person who died. How easy was it for me to pretend that their loved one's death did not happen at all. How naive was it for me to tell them, "just text and call if you want to talk," and believe they had to be the one to initiate. Instead of taking the time to investigate how I could help them, I did my part by leaving it up to them. It is exhausting to grieve and then have to muster the courage to let someone know you want to talk about difficult things. If someone just asked how I felt, the words would come out so much more easily than if I asked someone to listen.

However, there really are no rules when it comes to grieving. I liked the silence in the beginning, but later, it felt like an insult, like I was being ignored. I'll admit, the tricky part is knowing when it shifts: when the silence is needed and when it is rude.

Another place my words made it to the surface was through social media. When something triggers my grief, a rush of thoughts and memories start filling my head until they burst out in the form of lengthy and sporadic posts about my mother. I could not keep these words to myself. I needed to satisfy my grief by letting the whole world know how much I missed my mother by displaying it on the world wide web. I needed people to know that my mother was once alive and is now gone, even if they never met her. If people knew how much I wanted her back, then she continues to exist out in the world and not only in my memories.

Most of all, I did not want people to think that I handled my grief well.

Initially, when people told me, "You're very brave, you are so strong," or "I could never go through what you went through," I didn't think much of what they said. Sooner or later, their words started to bother me, making me feel uncomfortable the more I chewed on them in my head over and over again.

One of my friends told me that it was like I disappeared for a month after my mother passed away and then suddenly showed up at our usual coffee shop, ready to hang out. I came back to my normal routine and habits as if I didn't experience the most life-altering change, as if I didn't just undergo the most traumatic period of my entire life, as if I didn't see the person I loved slowly die for months.

Is crying and anger the only way to grieve? Do I have to sob every time I talk about my mother? Do I have to make drastic changes in my life for my pain to be evident?

It's complicated. I wanted to pretend everything was the same, but I also wanted my friends to see through that, to notice that things really weren't. But, I never got an indication of that, just them taking my lead and never asking.

My mother died. How could I be okay even if I appeared the same on the outside? People thought I handled my grief well because I didn't act how they imagined a grieving person would. This is where my loneliness started sinking in. I felt as if my friends couldn't see who I really was anymore. The person they knew had gone through the biggest change in her entire life, and all they could see was the same person from before. I was completely changed underneath; pieces of me were shifting to adjust to the grief that had lodged itself firmly in my core. I was different, and no one could see that. Or maybe they could, but they never said anything.

So, I had to let people know that I wasn't the same person anymore. I had to let people know that I was grieving, because if I let them believe I handled my grief well, then what does that say about my mother's life? What does that say about my mother's love for me? I had to let people know that my mother's absence made a difference to me, that her life mattered so much to me.

My mother exchanged her presence for my grief when she died. It was what I had of her. Every time someone told me I was brave or courageous and that I handled it well, I felt like they were tearing my grief apart, piece by piece until I would be left with nothing. I had to do something to stop my grief from being destroyed, to protect what my mother left me. So, I did what I usually do when I am upset: I wrote down everything I felt.

When I saw all my feelings materialize in a post, I felt lighter. After examining the words carefully and picturing how people would respond to it, a voice emerged from my thoughts and asked, "Are you sure you want to post it? Isn't it enough that you know how you felt? Do you really want to let others know? Do you really have to go that far?" I didn't want to be that person on social media who overshared, who took up too much space on someone's newsfeed, and who put herself publicly in the world and didn't receive a response. I didn't want to create another opportunity for me to be ignored. My pride always found a way to make things more difficult and delayed.

I had to remind myself that I wasn't doing this for the "likes;" I just needed a space to be seen and heard. The grief that was wedged so deeply inside of me was yearning to come out. It needed air, and I needed to help it breathe. Thinking about how trapped my grief was, I clicked the post button. Unlike the real world where I was met with silence for sharing about my mother, I receive a virtual applause and celebration in the form of social media currency: likes, hearts, and comments.

I'll admit, I originally liked getting the likes. It was a relief to be validated, to know people saw what I wrote, for people to know that I was still grieving. After the appeal of the likes wore off, the suspicion of being misunderstood returned through reading the comments. I felt like I was back to square one, as if people were now buying even more into this idea that I was brave for grieving out loud. Once again, people thought I was being strong.

I wasn't strong, I wasn't brave. I was a coward.

Even though I mentioned my mother often in conversations, it is not the same as talking about grief. Although your loved one who passed and the grief you've experienced as a result are connected, they are two separate things. I couldn't find the courage to share in person what my grief felt like, so I decided to write about it, to at least get the words out even if I couldn't find the courage to say them out loud.

When people heard that I was writing a memoir on grief, they told me how brave I was for writing about something so deep and personal. I still can't help but feel that they are wrong about me. People calling me brave makes me feel as if I am handling my grief in some unique, powerful way. Really, I think I am experiencing grief in the way that most people do.

Being called brave for going through something that will happen to everyone sounds ridiculous to me. You are not brave or courageous for going through grief; you are enduring. Grief is the hard labor of confronting the truth that you do not want to accept but must face every day. It is the revelation of how mortal and imperfect we are. It is the life experience of the truth that we cannot escape: all things must end. Everything you love will die.

Including you, reader.

Death is bound to happen to us all. Grief is really not that remarkable. It is the most ordinary experience that we will go through, the most certain thing to happen to all of us. Yet, we are so afraid of it. When we see others that recently lost someone, we tell ourselves that it's better to not bring it up and intrude on their grief. We become so paralyzed by our own insecurities about interacting with the grieving person that we avoid the topic altogether, convincing ourselves that it is better if we don't bring it up. There is less effort in assuming we know the answer rather than taking the time to investigate and see if it is true.

It is so much easier believing that what we say will only make it worse and that it is better to leave them alone. Why bother untangling something we don't know anything about? Leave them to it. We can help but only if they ask. It may seem as if we are being considerate of the grievers by giving them all the space they need, but in reality, we are considering our own needs and how we want to handle the situation. If we really wanted to find out how best to comfort a person, we would ask instead of assuming we know.

Once, I heard someone ask, "Where are the days when people used to bring casseroles when someone died?" A few weeks earlier, I heard someone on a podcast about grief ask, "Why do people keep bringing me food after my loss? Why do they think that I want them to make me dinner?"

There is no right way to respond to a grieving person. Everyone needs different things—sometimes money for the funeral expenses, homemade dinner for a week, or a vacation to get away from everything. You won't know unless you ask.

If they want to be left alone, they will tell you (or not respond to you). If they are unsure, then you can help them find out what works best for them. And sometimes we can't provide any assistance because we live too far away or we just don't have the capacity or resources. But we still have our words, which is better than silence.

In the beginning, I wanted to be left alone. I didn't want to talk about my grief. I just wanted to wait for the days to pass until I was ready to return to the world. But I appreciated when people reached out to me, even if I didn't respond back.

I still remember the people who sent me flowers, cards, and gift cards from Amazon and my favorite coffee shop. One of my friends even asked me if she could donate to my mother's favorite charities. These things didn't make my grief any easier, but I felt comforted by the sincerity behind their gifts and messages. To this day, the lily plant my friends sent me is sitting in my living room. When I look at the lily plant, I think about how it has been alive for as long as my mother has been dead. Then I remember how I felt when I received the flowers and the other gifts: seen. Even though I didn't want to talk to or interact with anyone after my mother died, I still wanted my pain to be acknowledged.

It hurts when your loved one dies. And it hurts a little more when no one recognizes your pain.

But, I am speaking for myself. Maybe for others, they prefer not to receive messages or flowers. You have to find out for yourself what they want. If they want to be left alone, at least you know that is what they want; at least you tried.

So, friends, I'm not asking you to constantly ask how the grievers in your life are doing. I'm encouraging you to take the initiative, whether it's a more specific ask or sending a text or card—anything to acknowledge that you see what they are going through. Do not be afraid to find out how they want to be comforted. Don't assume you know how to support a grieving person or that you know what a grieving person wants. Everyone grieves in their own way.

And grief never stops. It weaves in and out of our lives depending on the events and circumstances. It also never looks the same. The grief we experience at the funeral, at a future milestone without them, or at their twenty-year death anniversary looks and feels different. Whether the pain is really fresh or is many years old, it is always nice having a friend in those moments. Grief doesn't leave you once it comes. It stays for as long as you love that person you miss. And with most people, that's until the very end.

Even though I have learned so much more about grief from my mother's passing, I am not an expert. I continue to find myself unsure of what to do when I talk to a grieving person. The old tendencies of wanting to avoid the conversation about their loved one and not reaching out are still there. I still find myself paralyzed with uncertainties and doubt when I encounter a bereaved person, but this time,

I am trying to push through that discomfort and be more bold and empathetic.

So, grievers, I hope you can be more kind and forgiving to those who have not experienced loss yet or did not respond well or at all to your grief. It is tempting to get upset at those who didn't reach out to us when we were grieving or who responded in a way that we didn't like.

Friends, forgive me if I sounded angry at the start of this chapter. When my mother first passed away, I didn't recognize the loneliness in me for more than a year. I don't think I truly understood the depth of my loneliness until I started writing this book. I am more upset at myself that it took so long for me to admit that I wanted to be checked in on or comforted. And sometimes I feel like it is too late, that no one wants to hear about my grief anymore because some time has passed. I am still grieving, and I just wanted to let people know.

This book is not the result of me being angry at people's lack of response. I wrote this book to bridge the gap between grievers and not-yet grievers.

Grievers, I know that it can be exhausting to have to be the one to start the conversation about grief. Even though it's nice that people are waiting for you to respond, they don't realize how much energy and courage it takes to say that we are ready to talk about it. I hope that doesn't discourage you from finding a way to connect and share your grief when you are ready. Since grief is so certain and so prevalent, we must find a way to mourn together because that is one place where hope lies—in each other. Even though death separates, it also connects. One day, they will experience loss, and it will be our turn to comfort them. We can use the grief we hold to be more patient, kind, and forgiving. Grief hurts, but it can heal.

And, I hope you won't contain your grief forever, that you will find a way to release it into the world in your own way. From my own loss, I have learned there is no appropriate way to grieve. Grief looks different for everyone, and everyone has a different way of expressing and unleashing it.

It took me a while to discover how I like to process my sorrow and what I wanted to do with all the thinking that goes behind it. For the longest time, I only knew how I didn't want to grieve—by not crying or talking about it. Eventually, I noticed how much freer I felt after I posted about my grief online. Sometimes, I have too many thoughts and feelings in my head that it is hard to see what is really true. Writing helps me decipher what I am currently feeling, whether it is true or not, and how my grief changes and evolves over time. I find that I understand myself better when I am able to lay out all my musings, memories, and introspection to examine and inspect. I've always found it fun to psychoanalyze myself and others.

When I was younger, I fell in love with reading through the *Harry Potter* series. I discovered how fun it was to escape into fantasy worlds, meet characters I would never come across in real life, explore places I could never go to. I love where reading took me. As I got older, my love for reading evolved. It was no longer a break from the real world, but it brought me to the thoughts of real people in this world. In college, I finally got around to reading C. S. Lewis's *Mere Christianity,* a favorite among many Christians. Whenever I came across something in the book that deeply resonated with me, the world suddenly felt less lonely because I found someone who understood what I felt in that moment, except he expressed it so much more eloquently and beautifully. This is the power of writing: the ability to connect people through time by stringing words together.

And that is what I hope to do with my grief: to connect briefly with others through space and time. Reader, even if we never meet, if you feel less lonely for a nanosecond because of my experiences, then all the energy and time I spent on this book will be worth it.

To all the grievers and soon-to-be grievers, whatever your medium, I hope you will find a way to use it to connect with others. Grief is all around us. It would be a shame to go through it alone. Have courage and see where your grief will lead you. Do not be afraid of the sorrow inside of you. Don't keep it buried within you forever. Let it out when you are ready, one word, song, or brush stroke at a time. Everyone has their own time.

My time is now.

ACKNOWLEDGMENTS

First, I would like to thank my mother for loving me so much. I'm sorry for everything I did and didn't do. I wish that I didn't have to write this memoir and that I didn't realize all the things I had to say until after you passed away. I miss you every day. I love you, and I know you loved me. Before I know, this world will pass me by. After all, we are all just a moment in time, "a mist that appears for a little time and then vanishes" (James 4:14). See you in heaven.

Next my dad, who probably won't read this book because I've never seen him read a book. Thank you for taking care of me well into my adulthood. I would not be able to survive without you sheltering me, driving me places, and filling my car with gas. I don't need to say what I feel because you already know it. I will try to go to sleep earlier. Okay, enough of the cringe-ness

Thank you to my aunt and grandma for raising and feeding me and who have shown me so much grace and patience while living with me. You two hold the pieces of my mother I cannot find anywhere else.

I couldn't find the place to share this in my memoir, but thank you to my best friend Kelsey Chen for coming to my house when my mother died and taking the time off work to plan my mother's funeral. I will always remember having you there. Thank you for your constant support in everything I do even if I don't listen to you, feeding me, and driving me places. Time after time, you always come through for me.

Huge shout out to my beta readers. Elizabeth Fang, I am so thankful for your consistent feedback and faithful friendship. Thank you so much for your time and commitment. I value your insight so much whether it is for this book, life, and most importantly, faith! Canada awaits us! Priscilla Kong, how I wish I asked you earlier to be my beta reader. For the chapters you didn't read, I find myself thinking, what changes would Priscilla make here? Have you considered being an editor? Because you would make a fantastic one. Lillian Eng, you clever girl! I know I can always count on you for being so punny. I wish you could name all the titles of my chapters. Thank you for your constant support and driving to my house. :) Steven Cheng and Micah Shyu, You guys rock! I appreciate every single comment and feedback you provided. Lilly Chang, I know, I'm sorry I should have replied back and helped you find a way to provide feedback. I'm sure it would have been great, but I figured your time is better spent preparing for your wedding. And Sonny Lai, I know you didn't get a chance to provide feedback, but I am still grateful for your interview and insight and just this awful way we are connected in how we lost our mothers around the same time.

Thank you to Jessie Cheng, author of *Unglamored*. The very first person to preorder my book and the person who introduced this program to me. Without you, I would have never published this book. But most of all, I needed to be inspired first by how much courage you took to write yours.

Thank you to New Degrees Press for giving me the opportunity to share my story with the world! Thank you: Professor Eric Koester, for not only creating this program but for making me realize that my book was about loneliness, the central theme of my memoir; Quinn Karrenbauer, for all the encouragement I needed at the beginning when I didn't even know where my book was headed; Olivia Bearden, for keeping me on track and making sure this book actually got published. I always look forward to your feedback.

Thank you to all my cousins who were so supportive during the preorder process and my mother's cancer and death. Melissa, Jessica, Christina, Melinda, Jordan, Brandon, and David: you're all incredibly special to me in your own way, and I enjoy every moment that I get to spend with you!

Also, I couldn't have written my book without the general support of my friends and community. These are the people and groups I love and belong to. HOC6, the place where all my growing pains of faith happened and the place where my heart continues to be time after time. #trendYAdult sg, the place I always want to be on Friday nights, your conversations enrich and refresh me, and this is really the best small group I have ever been a part of. The girls at 128—so much joy when God brings us all together. I could spend hours with you all; maybe that is why we don't see each other that often. (Haha.) Tiff Mikamo, your constant support in everything I do is immeasurable. Jendo, you know how to keep me grounded, and for that I am incredibly grateful. Kristi Chinn and Carissa Muljadi, every year I become more and more grateful for our long-lasting friendship, Estefania Guerreros, thank you for taking care of me throughout college and beyond; you are the friend that always has my back, and I hope you know I have yours too. Eunice Kung, I am constantly inspired by your thoughtfulness and care to those around you—so glad I get to be a part of that! Denise Lee, thank you for the real tough conversations and never-ending support. Joana Hsu, despite our distance, I love how often we get to talk! Devout Crew, without you all, I would be lonelier and less caffeinated. I hope we continue to meet now and in eternity. And the solid crew, most of the time you guys make me want to facepalm or roll my eyes, but I somehow always end up laughing.

And of course, to all the people who preordered my book, who believed in me when I didn't. I did not know I needed an authors' community to write a book. I thought I would be writing this book for myself, but I realized how much better it is to write with others in mind. You are the people I thought of when I couldn't get over my procrastination hurdle or writing slump. I wrote this with each one of you in mind; I hope you will enjoy the read! Thank you for teaching me that dreams don't belong to the dreamers but to those who believed in them. I am forever grateful.

Adele Cheng
Adrienne Cheng
Alexis Lozano
Alicia Lo
Alvina Yau
Alyssa Chan
Angela Hsu
Chelsie Gho
Cheryl Chiu
Christina Gin

Anh Truong
Anna Sit
Any Hsu
Brandon Ng
Carissa Muljadi
Caroline Chen
Caryn Medina
Cheryl Yu
Christina Chu
Frank Li

Christina Mei Chang
Christina Shiea
Christina Yu
Christopher and
Yiqin Thomas
Christopher Chiang
Cindy Yue Lau
Colette Young
Connie Lee
Daniel and Kelsey Chen
Darren and Elaine Lee
Denise Lee
Diana L
Doris Yau
Elaine Lai
Elizabeth Fang
Emily Chao
Emily Chen
Enoch Quon
Eric Chen
Eric Koester
Erik Teensma
Estefania Guerreros
Esther Lai
Eunice Kung
Kevin Quan
Kevin Taki
Kristi Chinn
Hannah Chen
Jabez L Bush
Jackie Lim
Janice E Ho
Jasmine Chan
Jennifer Do
Jennifer Kwon
Jessica Chang
Jessie Cheng
Jonathan Cheng
Jonathan Huang
Jonathan Luong
Jordan Kong
Joshua and Alanna Chen
Joshua Scott
Joshua Wong
Julia Kim
Julia Lau
Julie Huang
Julie Leadbetter
Justice Yen
Katie Martin
Katie Haverly
Kelly Chien
Philip Fang
Phillip Yoon
Priscilla Kong
Kyra Chan

Lea Le

Lillian Eng

Lilly-anne Hermosilla

Linda Kang

Luna Chang

Marion Eng

Matthew Mui

Megan Cheng

Megan Ma

Melanie Chow

Melinda Chang

Melissa Ng

Mia Griffin

Micah Shyu

Michael Yount

Michelle Ong

Miryam Ha

Moonkyung Kim

Nethen Mou

Oliver Yuan

Olivia Lam

Patrick C

Winnie Chang

Wiseley Fong

Rebecca Lum

Ryan Chao

Samantha Mar

Sandi Mar

Sarah Burger

Sarah Fong

Sole Chang

Sonny Lai

Stephanie Chang

Stephanie Wood

Steven Cheng

Tgliew

Tiffany Hendric Lee

Tiffany Lee

Tiffany Mikamo

Tirza White

Tracy Truong

Tsz Yu Chan

Valerie Andrews

Vivi Angelina

Wendy Chen

Wilson Chan

Winfield Zhang

Yalopez

Last, and most certainly not least, I cannot end my acknowledgments without acknowledging my Heavenly Father, who made all things possible! Everything that happened to me, who I am, and who I will be is all because of you. I am constantly learning that everything is temporary but you. You are everlasting.

APPENDIX

______

CHAPTER 1

Shankman, Adam, dir. *A Walk to Remember*. 2002; United States: Warner Bros. Pictures, 2002. DVD.

CHAPTER 3

Kim, Jin-won, dir. *Just Between Lovers*. Season 1, episode 13, aired January 22, 2018, on JTBC https://www.viki.com/videos/1123717v-just-between-lovers-episode-13.

CHAPTER 5

Ha, Byung-hoon, dir. *Go Back Couple*. Season 1, episode 1, aired October 13, 2017, on KBS2 https://www.kocowa.com/en_us/media/226372/go-back-couple-episode-1.

Ha, Byung-hoon, dir. *Go Back Couple*. Season 1, episode 8, aired October 13, 2017, on KBS2 https://www.kocowa.com/en_us/media/226372/go-back-couple-episode-8.

CHAPTER 6

Kondo, Marie. *The Life-Changing Magic of Tidying Up: The Japanese Art of Decluttering and Organizing. Tokyo*: Sunmark Publishing, 2011.

Wallis, Jade Sandberg, dir. *Tidying Up with Marie Kondo*. Season 1, episode 4, "Sparking Joy After a Loss." Aired January 1, 2019, on Netflix. https://www.netflix.com/watch/80209467?trackId=13752289.

CHAPTER 7

Wilkinson, Dawn dir. *Kim's Convenience*. Season 1, episode 10, "Janet's New Job." Aired December 13, 2016 on CBC. https://www.netflix.com/watch/80209467?trackId=13752289.

Perfect Goodbyes. "Cemetery Burial Plot Cost in California: Cheapest and Most Expensive Options (2021)." Accessed October 16, 2021. https://www.perfectgoodbyes.com/california-cemetery-burial-plot-costs/.